Endorsements

"One of the things I love about the author is the depth and authenticity she displays as she shares her story of abuse; she is real, and her story is very relatable for victims of domestic violence. Her genuineness has the power to break the chains of darkness experienced by the abused. In her new book she brings a rather unique modality to dealing with and healing the pain of adversity -twelve impactful devotional testimonies about how she discovered and utilized the power of prayer. *"…relying on the Problem Solver and not focusing on the problem."* This book is riveting; it is a must read. Thanks, Fiona!"

–Dr. Sonia M. Smith, Founder and Director of Family Matters Counseling and Consulting Services

"*24 Days: Prayer to the Rescue Series* is a remarkable read. Each chapter shows the importance of prayer and what happens when we pray. It reveals that prayer is important and we are wealthy when it is a part of our lives."

–Hollis A. Charles, Sr. Hospital Care Investigator

"I was truly awed by reading Ms. Harewood's book, *24 Days - Prayer to the Rescue*. It chronicles real life events about how, through earnest and sometimes even simple prayer and supplication to God, miraculous things can happen in our lives. They ranged from those as major as the saving of lives, the restoration of a marriage, and protection during a storm, to having the key to unlock a door, all with the understanding that God sometimes says "No." The book is not only an inspiration to those who are ready to end their marriages; it assures us that if we pray without ceasing God will come through for us – if it's His will – no matter how great or small the request is."

–Tanya Bloomfield, Assistant Principal

"To truly understand the "Power of Prayer" you must experience it; only then will you have the authority to expound on it. The author shared her lived experiences with fervor. This narrative is guaranteed to change lives and give hope to anyone who is challenged by life's crucibles."

–Denese Clue, Deputy Assistant Director

24 DAYS

PRAYER to the RESCUE

A SERIES BY **FIONA HAREWOOD**

BOOK ONE

24 Days

Prayer to the Rescue

A Series by
FIONA HAREWOOD

Hope Publishers

We Empower! You Overcome!

24 Days is a compilation of individual testimonies.

Unless otherwise indicated, all Bible references are taken from the New King James Version®. Copyright© 1982 by Thomas Nelson. Used by permission. All rights reserved.

Scripture quotations from the Authorized (King James) Version. Rights in the Authorized Version in the United Kingdom are vested in the Crown. Reproduced by permission of the Crown's patentee. Cambridge University Press.

All the stories related in this book are true, but some of the names have been changed or omitted to protect the privacy of the people mentioned.

24 Days: Prayer to the Rescue
Copyright© 2022 by Fiona Harewood. All rights reserved.
Printed in the United States of America
Published by Hope Publishers

All rights reserved. This book contains material protected under International and Federal Copyright Laws and Treaties. Any unauthorized reprint or use of this material is prohibited. No part of this book may be reproduced or transmitted in any form or by any means, electronic or mechanical, including photocopying, recording, or by any information storage and retrieval system, without express written permission from the author.

Identifiers:
Library of Congress Control Number: 2022909655
ISBN: 978-0-9838774-2-4 (paperback)
ISBN: 978-0-9838774-3-1 (ebook)

Any Internet addresses (websites, blogs, etc.) and telephone numbers printed in this book are offered as a resource. They are not intended in any way to be or imply an endorsement by Hope Publishers, nor does Hope Publishers vouch for the content of these sites and numbers for the life of this book.

Book cover designed by Raman Bhardwaj

Also by Fiona Harewood

I DID IT . . . YOU CAN TOO!
View book trailer and receive a free excerpt at:
https://fionaharewood.com/i-did-it-you-can-too/

*RIVER NEVER SMOOTH:
RECLAIMING POWER AFTER ABUSE*
View book trailer and receive a free excerpt at:
https://fionaharewood.com/river-never-smooth/

"Self-Love: The Key To Successful Relationships"
(The Pandemic Within A Pandemic)

View Trailer & Introduction to this ***online course*** here:
https://fionaharewood.com/online-course/

YouTube Channel here:

youtube.com/c/FionaHarewoodHopePublishers

DEDICATION

In loving memory of my best friend,
the late June Ann Reid
You epitomized the servant leader.

Contents

Foreword xiii
Introduction xv

Part I: My Warfare Mode of Prayers

One – Still in the Saving Business. 2
Two – The Devil's Agenda – to Kill us . . . BUT GOD!. 16
Three – 24 Days 26

Part II: My Perseverance Mode of Prayers

Four – An Immigrant's Story 60
Five – The Day He Blessed and Made Holy 86
Six – Faith in Action! 100

Part III: My Relaxed Mode of Prayers

Seven – Shelter in a Storm 108
Eight – $2.00 Multiplied More Than 100 Times. 116
Nine – Turn the Doorknob! 122
Ten – Hidden From Their 'Eyes' 128
Eleven – Even Before I Prayed .136
Twelve – "Pick up the Receiver" 144

Acknowledgements. 149
About the Author. 151

Foreword

Every great story has a hero! In the book you are now holding, *24 Days: Prayer to the Rescue,* Fiona Harewood shares some unbelievable stories. The personal experiences she relates are incredible, inspiring, and even miraculous. Yet, more significantly, they are also true. I know this because of my personal acquaintance with the author, and because I am a first-hand witness to some of the events she describes. But although told by Fiona, this book really isn't about her. She is not the heroine. The hero of the story is the God who has revealed Himself in the pages of the Bible.

In *24 Days: Prayer to the Rescue*, God is revealed as the great Problem-Solver and through the real-life experiences it describes, we discover that prayer is the avenue by which God is *invited* to become involved in our lives. In fact, in the Bible, God is repeatedly inviting us to allow Him to help us in our circumstances. "Then call on me when you are in trouble, and I will rescue you, and you will give me glory" (Psalm 50:15 NLT). God says call on Me – that is pray to Me – when you are in trouble, and I will deliver you. That is *Prayer to the Rescue*!

I believe the testimonies shared in this book will build your faith in God. I have found that prayer and faith are inseparable. They are like Siamese twins—you cannot see one without seeing the other. If we believe in God and believe that He is able to solve our problems, then we will be encouraged to call on Him, and ask Him to handle whatever we're dealing with.

As you journey through this book, you will find that the Hero of these stories restores broken relationships, pays college tuition, defies disease, tells the truth, locates the things we have lost, and overturns governmental systems. He is the God who opens closed doors and makes a way when there seems to be no way!

It is these experiences that convince us that God, indeed, is good, and persuades us to trust Him. This is so important because while God answers every prayer, He does not always answer at the time or in the way we anticipate. We need the faith to believe that God is trustworthy even when He chooses not to answer our prayers in the way we had hoped. The Hero of this story is a wise and loving Father and just as a child trusts her parent, without being able to fully understand why he sometimes tell her "No," we too can trust that God's heart only desires what is best for us.

Along with the author, I pray that *24 Days: Prayer to the Rescue* will lead you to realize that we can trust God in every situation.

–Donald C. McKinnie, Jr., DMin.

Senior Pastor

Introduction

"CAN'T YOU SEE I'M ON THE PHONE?" I screamed over the sound of the radio my husband was blasting. He knew quite well that I had just begun a conversation with a sister from my church. Shouting those words resulted in *war!* Before that moment, our lives were like a ticking time bomb. My current husband, Paul, was my third, and yet I still hadn't found my *happily ever after*. Instead of living harmoniously and enjoying each other, the chasm between us widened each day. While I enjoyed going to church and serving the Lord, Paul didn't care much for that part of my life. We were living under the same roof but leading separate lives.

If things didn't change soon, our marriage would be over. I couldn't continue in this unhappy relationship, especially when it seemed as though I was the only one who was trying to make the marriage work. The next day – my 54th birthday – I woke up deciding that I wasn't going to do it anymore. *It would be better to do bad all by myself,* I thought. I stuffed most of my clothes and personal items into my car and drove to a friend's house. I didn't really want to end my marriage, but I felt that drastic measures needed to be taken.

My husband was stubborn, so it made no sense trying to reason with him. Before going to bed that night, I called Paul at his job.

"When you get home, I will not be there, and I will not be coming back. Ever." There was a pregnant pause at the other end of the line. When he finally answered, his voice had lost some of its bravado.

"What are you saying? I don't understand," he said.

"I've tried long and hard to keep this marriage together, but it is not working. I turned 54 years old today and I am not going to spend the rest of my life being miserable and unhappy. I've had enough. Goodnight." Powering off my cell phone, I retired for the evening.

That night, I laid in bed thinking about all the problems Paul and I were encountering in our marriage. I felt helpless and didn't believe anything could make our situation better. Eventually, I prayed, talking to God about our marriage and about us. After praying, I laid, silently thinking. Then something hit me. Have you ever experienced one of those *aha moments?* Well, I had one of those moments. It was the recognition of that moment – which I will share with you later – that changed everything. After acting based on that realization, I had my husband and my marriage back within a week. That awareness became the basis of this book.

For the most part, sustaining a marriage is challenging. Distractions can create more tension in a relationship that may already be fraying around the edges. They may take the form of sophisticated women and attractive men vying for attention at the workplace; after-work bars; or the many business trips taken without the spouse or partner. Financial pressures, the illness of a spouse, or the demands of one's job, can also disrupt harmony in relationships. Just as it is necessary to nurture our children, attend to our health, and plan for our future, we need to continuously work at our relationships. If neither party cares, nor seeks to strengthen the relationship, it may eventually break down – perhaps even become irreparable. Similarly, in every situation with which we are confronted, our actions determine the outcome.

According to the article, "Divorce Statistics and Facts in the United States," every 13 seconds, someone, somewhere, files for divorce.[1] The article cites eight years as the average life span of a first

---

[1] Divorce Statistics and Facts in the United States https://www.divorcelawyers-formen.com/blog/divorce-rate-us-2018/

marriage and notes that 66% of divorce filings are made by women. Further, statistics revealed 639,000 divorce filings in the United States in 1969, with that number almost doubling ten years later to 1,181,000. While there seems to have been a decline in the divorce rate in the 2000's, experts believe that this is attributable to fewer people getting married as opposed to longer lasting unions as folks were either living alone or cohabitating more.

I wanted my marriage to last, but I was tired of being tired. So, while in bed at my friend's house, I thought about our marriage and all the remedies I had tried to make things better. I thought about friends who had shared with me their attempts to heal their own broken marriages. It seemed as if we were all suffering from a critical flaw in how we tried to hold our marriages together or solve the major problems that confronted us. As a matter of fact, even those whose marriages could be considered almost perfect still needed to learn that secret.

As I mentioned earlier, restoring my marriage was one of the outcomes I anticipated after my *aha moment*. Having found the answer for which most people were searching, I began coaching others about how to deal not only with marital problems, but also with other life's difficulties. This was made possible because of the remarkably simple insight I discovered while talking to God about Paul, our marriage, and myself. Since then, I have noticed that regardless of the situation in which my husband and I find ourselves, whether it be coping with illness, grieving the death of loved ones, or navigating financial hardship, we are able to handle these problems so much better than we could previously.

This book presents a startlingly simple but often overlooked fact that will transform how you deal with any problem or difficulty, despite what life throws at you. When faced with problems, if we are honest, many of us would have to admit that our first line of defense is to turn to a friend or family member for advice. At other times, we concoct our own solutions which may involve thinking inside the box and this prevents us from really grasping the bigger picture. We may trust in ourselves—relying on our own strength, our finances, or our spouses, but we soon learn that these things are grossly insufficient.

For instance, how many of us wake up in the morning deciding to fully consecrate ourselves and our day to God? And although we may do that, how many times negative and unexpected situations invade our lives, disappointing and frustrating us because we are not wholly grounded in God and His Word? This is not a new dynamic; even the Biblical characters whom we learn about and to whom we often look have had to deal with the same challenges.

For example, in Genesis chapter 29, the Bible recounts the story of Jacob, Rachel, and Leah, a saga which would put any modern-day soap opera to shame. Rachel envied her sister because, unlike Leah, she was barren. Both sisters were married to Jacob – the result of their father, Laban's scheme to get 14 years of free labor from his unsuspecting son-in-law. Because the culture of the time dictated that the older daughter marries first, Laban swapped Rachel out for Leah on Jacob's wedding night.

Rachel spent an abundance of time focusing on her problem and applying incorrect methods to solve it. She grew tired of watching her sister bear children while she could not. So, she decided, in her own strength, to do something about it. First, she demanded that her husband give her children, adding, "or else I die," Genesis 30:1. Of course, granting that wish was way above Jacob's pay grade. In her desperate quest to become a mother, Rachel encouraged her husband to give her a child via her handmaid/servant. She even struck a deal with Leah to score some mandrakes (an herb believed to boost fertility) which she planned to use in the hope of increasing her chances of becoming pregnant – to no avail. Eventually, God in His mercy opened Rachel's womb and she bore two sons.

Similarly, to Rachel, in my marriage, I focused on the problems. I know I am not unique in this regard because generally, when confronted with most of life's challenges, people tend to do the same. After realizing the solution to my marital problems, I stopped trying to fix them in the conventional fashion. I didn't call Paul and try to make up with him; I didn't tell people what was going on, nor did

I worry. Instead, I became still, took my eyes off the problems, and depended on God. If He was going to fix them, He certainly didn't need my help.

We falsely assume that concentrating on our problems, relying on our own strength, and creating our own solutions are effective forms of mitigation. However, the *ah ha moment* of realization I mentioned above, revealed a simple truth: **Our problems are solved when we focus, not on the problems, but on the Problem Solver.** 1 Peter 5:7 reminds us to cast all our care upon Him because He cares for us. Proverbs 3:5-6 tells us "Trust in the Lord with all your heart and lean not on your own understanding; In all your ways acknowledge Him, and He shall direct your paths." When you focus on the *Problem Solver* instead of on your problems, you will be well on your way to experiencing transformation in your life. This change will emerge whether the revolution you seek is in restoring your marriage, like I did with Paul, (refer to chapter 1); whether we must launch out in faith and see how He opens doors for us, (refer to chapter six); instead of worrying when you are caught in a storm, call on Him and see how He shows up miraculously, (refer to chapter 7); whether you need a quarter to make a call at a pay phone, (See chapter 12); and in every troublesome or trying situation, we must petition God, take our eyes off the problem, and watch Him work. See how He kept my lost wallet hidden from eyes, (refer to chapter 10).

For the most part, we care about our problems and how to eradicate the pain that results from them. However, our conventional wisdom fails us, creating unnecessary stress. After learning that I needed to allow the *Problem Solver* to do His work in my life, I decided to let go and allow God to take charge. That's when I saw results! That's when the *Problem Solver* stepped in and turned my marriage around in such a phenomenal way that even today, people continue to marvel, and I cease not to be amazed.

Throughout the next twelve chapters of this book, I will share the details of these real-life stories of how my family, and I focused on the *Problem Solver* – God Himself – instead of directing our minds to devastating situations that threatened to destroy us. You will see how God stepped in and turned circumstances around. My hope is that you too, will learn to trust Him in your dilemmas.

In this book, I have shared my three modes of prayer: my warfare, perseverance, and relaxed iterations. My warfare method illustrates how I prayed when life threw curve balls that knocked my family and me off our feet and left us reeling. This method helped us claim the victory over any situation despite the apparent odds, while still allowing the *Problem Solver* – and *not* the problem – to be the focus. My perseverance mode reveals how life can sometimes take a negative turn creating situations that plague us and cause us to question our faith. These situations appear protracted regardless of how much we pray. To be victorious I describe how I persevered in the face of adversity, relying on the *Problem Solver*, and not focusing on the problem. For my relaxed mode, I share stories set when life's seas were calm. There were no fierce trials and when situations arose sometimes God stepped in and answered before I even prayed.

Introducing every chapter is a devotional thought designed to help you prove for yourself what God says in His Word regarding the circumstances I describe. The stories that follow are real encounters I have had with God which I trust will help your faith in Him to become stronger.

In this world, where the battle between good and evil is constantly raging, we are bombarded with scores of problems every day. Conventional theories don't solve our problems; focusing on them cannot produce the results we desire. Although there is a lot of noise through which we must navigate, as you gain insight into how the *Problem Solver* works – through His Word and real-life testimonies – and apply His Word to your life, you will marvel at the astounding metamorphosis.

PART I

My Warfare Mode of Prayers

*This method illustrates how I prayed along with others when life threw curve balls that knocked my family and me off our feet and left us reeling.
Ty Gibson, pastor and speaker/director for Light Bearers said that prayer is an act of war in The Great Controversy between good and evil.*

CHAPTER ONE

Call upon me in the day of trouble:
I will deliver you and you shall glorify me.

Psalm 50:15

What a promise! In His Word the Lord tells us to call on Him when we're in trouble, and not only will He deliver us, but we will praise Him. The Hebrew word for trouble is *akar*, which means to stir up or disturb. Trouble can refer to any difficulty a person is facing, and it takes many forms in our daily lives. A parent may experience trouble with a child who decides to experiment with drugs; an employee may have to deal with a challenging supervisor; a Christian husband may be at an impasse with his wife who doesn't think it necessary to put Christ first in their lives. Sickness, death, starvation, and financial hardships are all forms of trouble. At the time of this writing, the Coronavirus created yet another kind of trouble.

This means that everyone can relate to the word 'trouble' but although it touches us all at one time or another the ways in which it impacts us personally, may not be the same. Also, we may not all deal with it in the same way. The common denominator, however, is that through His Word, God is saying to all of us that we should call on Him in every situation. This includes when the kids are acting up, when the spouse is uncooperative, when the boss is being difficult, and when we are tried by sickness. We can call on Him when we're battered by the pain of losing a loved one, and even when debt collectors are continuously calling but there's no money to offer. Once you classify a situation as *trouble*, it's time to call on God.

God tells us to bring all our troubles or problems to Him and He *will* deliver us! He doesn't say, "I will *try* to help you." He doesn't make bringing our troubles to Him conditional. He simply says, "Tell me about your troubles." He then promises to deliver us. Now, when this deliverance occurs, it will be in such a distinct way that we will know that God intervened. Those looking on who witness our deliverance will know, undeniably, that it wasn't our doing but the divine intervention of the Supernatural One. God assures us that after He delivers us, we will have no alternative but to glorify Him – praise Him – and testify of what He has done!

Still in the Saving Business

It's Sunday, February 28, 2016 – a day I will *never* forget. Something I have desired for years, and for which I have been petitioning God, has been answered!

I have been praying for my husband's salvation for fifteen years and now it has happened. I am simply awed at what God has done and I cannot keep this wonderful news to myself. I must tell others because I know there are many wives praying for their husbands, and vice versa, countless parents praying for their children, and children praying for their parents. Overall, people everywhere are praying that loved ones be prepared to greet Jesus when He comes back for us. I am chronicling my experience to encourage you to persist in prayer. God will answer! He is kind like that! Further, it is not His will that any should perish but that we all will come to know and love Him and live with Him eternally (2 Pet. 3:9).

Prayer means a lot to me and when God answers my prayers – particularly given the fact that I am imperfect – I love to tell others of what He has done. And He has done it even for me! One of the requests I frequently made of God, was that He would save my husband. I told the Lord that I would brag on Him to the world via my testimonies, but I want to start this book with the testimony that is perhaps the one that is nearest and dearest to me – a testimony of His saving grace. I told Him I would start my book of testimonies when He saved my husband, making it the first testimony I would record as I share what He has done for me. For us. Well, God came through, and now, I am about to testify!

You may wonder why I wanted God to save my husband. Didn't I love him as he was? Aren't spouses supposed to be there *for better or for worse . . .?* Wasn't I supposed to accept my husband as he was? I'm not even sure how to answer those questions. What I do know is that it's difficult for two people to live harmoniously if they lead separate lives. Amos 3:3 asks a question: Can two walk together, except they agree? My husband, Paul, and I were not *walking together* and life in our home was getting progressively worse. We quarreled a lot, didn't speak to each other for extended periods of time, and frequently left the house without notifying each other.

My initial meeting with Paul was unique. We met on a flight between New York and Barbados. As a member of the airline staff, I recall boarding the aircraft last. Almost every space for baggage storage was taken and without me even having to ask, Paul got up and helped me make room for my carry-on. Being tired after a weekend of shopping, it seemed as though I fell asleep as soon as I sat down. He probably knew I was hungry because when I awoke, I discovered that he had saved me the lunch the flight attendant had brought. We began chatting and discovered that his family lived two blocks from where I lived in Barbados. During his month-long vacation, we became friends. At that time, I was clinging to a toxic relationship I knew I needed to end, but didn't – or rather, couldn't.

Paul and I kept in contact even when he returned to the United States. I didn't realize that he had fallen in love with me from the moment he saw me, until about six months later when I shared that the loser, I had been holding on to dumped me.

"I was waiting patiently for this moment because I knew it would happen," he said. "I held back because I wanted you to see for yourself that he didn't love you."

Our relationship blossomed. I was a Christian before meeting Paul, but I had stopped attending church regularly. A few years later, at Paul's invitation, my children and I moved to the United States, and we began living together. It's hard turning your back on God when you used to serve him faithfully. So, during my first year in the United States, I felt the need to rededicate my life to the Lord and to try living for Him. It was difficult being a Christian and living with a man to whom I wasn't married. That is fornication – a sin the Bible condemns, so after living together for two years, Paul and I got married.

We still loved each other but we began growing apart because I wanted to live for God, while Paul said he wanted nothing to do with church and the life I had chosen to live. His surface excuse was that people in the church were hypocrites. So, the separate paths we traveled created increased tension between us.

As time passed, we enjoyed each other less and less. And I say *we* because even though *I* was the Christian, I did things that may have contributed to his negative reactions. For instance, I had a bad temper – one that caused my pitch to escalate dramatically when I became angry. My husband couldn't stand that. Even my children became annoyed when I shouted at them. This was one of the things I had been praying about for years, asking God to deliver me from that angry spirit. There were times when I felt I was over it and then something would really upset me, and I would begin to scream. I believe that God has been working on that area of my life over the years, because I am doing much better now. Well, amongst other issues, it was one of those bouts of shouting that almost brought our marriage to a premature end.

I won't blame Paul for the breakdown in our marriage. The blame should be shared. My marriage to Paul was my third – a fact in which I take no pride. People talk about taking "baggage" into relationships. Well, Paul and I both had our share. Our marriage was Paul's second, and we both had children from our previous relationships.

Time passed and it seemed as though circumstances conspired to create tension between us at every turn. It frequently felt as though we were always arguing over one thing or another. Quarrels ranged from financial issues to him feeling like my kids – who lived with us – were not respectful enough. He even got upset when I was on the phone and complained that I spent too much time at church. We quarreled because I felt that he didn't spend any time with me, didn't take me anywhere anymore, and spent too much time with his friends. The list was endless.

Our lives continued along this downward spiral for years. Eventually my three children graduated from college, found jobs out of state, and moved on. Paul and I were now empty nesters – home alone. Unfortunately, things between us didn't change. In fact, they grew progressively worse. We slept in the same bed but that was about it. As I watched my husband drift away, I drew closer to God and more than ever I began praying that God would save him and allow us to live fulfilled lives in Him. Together.

When I attended Wednesday night prayer meetings, in addition to any other prayer requests I had, there was always one constant petition: "God, please save Paul." My heart was also warmed when my sister-in-law revealed that she rose at 5:00 a.m. every morning to pray for her brothers. I even began reading books that taught Christian wives how to treat their unsaved husbands, as another of my sisters-in-law gifted me with a copy of Stormie Omartian's, *The Power of a Praying Wife*.

Then, one day, the film, *War Room*, was shown at church. I settled in to watch it without expectations, but halfway through the story I began crying uncontrollably. I was so overwhelmed that one of my friends had to accompany me from the room. I couldn't continue watching. There was one scene in which Ms. Clara – one of the characters – encouraged Mrs. Jordan, the protagonist, to pray for her husband, even though Mrs. Jordan suspected that he was being unfaithful. It was as if Ms. Clara were telling the faithful wife that she would be the unfaithful one, creating trouble in her marriage if she didn't pray for, and forgive her husband. At that point I was through. It seemed to me as though a husband is allowed to do whatever he pleases while his wife is obligated to pray for him, and I just couldn't wrap my mind around that. I think that's when something within me shifted, and I stopped praying for Paul. I didn't make the effort to see the movie in its entirety until my husband surrendered his life to the Lord. Now, I am thankful for all the "Ms. Claras" out there.

Now, let me tell you about the shouting match I alluded to in the introduction. It was February 21, 2016, the day before my 54th birthday – a typical Sunday. I was preparing to attend a board meeting at my church when my phone rang. Paul was lying in bed listening to the radio. As I began speaking, he turned the volume on the radio up so loudly, that it was virtually impossible for me to properly hear what the person on the other end of line was saying. I quickly ended the call.

"CAN'T YOU SEE I'M ON THE PHONE?" I screamed over the sound of the radio. War broke out between us immediately after I shouted those words. To end the argument, I eventually left the bedroom and went to the bathroom. Paul followed me, shouting, and when I tried to leave the bathroom, he blocked my exit. At that point, I began screaming at him again, becoming so irate that I slammed my fist against the ceramic countertop which housed the bathroom sink. The screaming match continued, and a few minutes later, Paul also pounded on the countertop, emphasizing *his* point. The argument intensified. Although neither of us hit the countertop again, we watched in disbelief as it – and the sink – split into four pieces: two pieces on the left side, including the basin, and two pieces on the right side. Our screaming immediately stopped, both of us struggling to process what had just happened. In our rage, we had demolished the bathroom sink. The reality was sobering. It was at this point that the shouting ceased, and Paul stepped aside, allowing me to leave the bathroom. Neither of us said anything to the other for the rest of that day.

After Paul's conversion, he said that the bizarre breaking of the sink served as a warning that something bad could happen which was why he had stopped arguing with me.

That night I reasoned: *Tomorrow I will be 54; I've had two previous marriages, and neither worked, so why would this one work? Why am I wasting my life and time with someone who doesn't care about me? My kids are grown and on their own; I don't have to put up with this anymore. While I have time, I'm going to get out of this marriage.* I was determined not to spend another day stuck in a marriage that simply wasn't working. I deserved better. And yes, I was tired of praying for Paul.

The next day was Monday, February 22nd. It was my birthday, but, sadly, nothing special. My husband didn't remember it, which wasn't unusual, as it was never his practice to recognize or celebrate special days. At one time that would upset me, but it no longer does.

Now I find it funny, and giggle at the guilt that clouds his face when he realizes that he has missed an important milestone and tries hard to make up for it.

Later that day, after Paul left for work. I packed whatever clothes and personal items I could fit in my car and sought refuge at a friend's home, with the intention of finding an apartment quickly thereafter.

That night before I went to bed, I called Paul.

"When you get home, I will not be there, and I will not be coming back. Ever." There was a pregnant pause at the other end of the line. When he finally answered, his voice had lost some of its bravado.

"What are you saying? I don't understand," he said.

"I've tried long and hard to keep this marriage together, but it is not working. I turned 54 today and I am not going to spend the rest of my life being miserable and unhappy. I've had enough. Goodnight." Powering off my cell phone, I retired for the evening.

Although I was tired, sleep refused to come. Tossing and turning, I tried to pray but just couldn't find the words to say to God. Eventually, I decided to be honest with the Lord. Although He knew how I felt – because God knows everything – He still wanted me to talk to Him because He likes communicating with me and hearing from me. He's like that with you too – with all of us.

Lord, I began, *You know this is not what I want. I do not want to be here at my friend's house. Paul and I have our own home. Lord, I want to be at our home, in our bed. I need my husband. I want us to get along; I want us to start over; I want our marriage to work. Please God, fix this . . .* At some point I fell asleep.

Tuesday and Wednesday of that week were uneventful. I knew Paul could be very stubborn, so I wasn't even expecting to hear from him. I began searching for apartments and making plans to move out of my friend's house. Although I started praying again for Paul and our marriage, I didn't say too much to God. The most I said sometimes was, "Lord, please fix this." Many times, when I am weighed down by difficult circumstances, it's hard to find the words to pray and when I do pray, it's usually the one liner: "Lord you gotta fix this!" Or, like I prayed about my marriage, "Lord, please fix this."

Sometimes I even say, "Lord help!" or "Mercy, God!" This is my perseverance mode of prayer in its simplest form. If it worked for Peter, I figure it could work for me, too.

Around 9:00 a.m. on Thursday, February 25th, my phone lit up, displaying Paul's name. I was at work. I watched the ring signal for a few moments before I swiped.

"Hello."

"Fiona, it's not the same without you here." Paul sounded defeated and sad. I didn't respond. "With you not being here, I had a lot of time to think." I still didn't respond.

"I keep thinking of you, crying a lot, wishing you would come back. I even prayed to God, asking Him to let you come back. After I prayed, I remembered what my mother used to say to me when I was a boy. She used to say, *don't let me have to search heaven in vain for you*. I haven't thought about those words in years but in worrying about us, her words came right back to me, and they are still with me . . . Are you still there?"

"Yes."

"I would like to speak with your pastor. Can you make an appointment for me to see him?

"No. If you want to see him, make the appointment yourself."

"But I don't have his number."

"Here it is," I said, repeating the number slowly so he could write it down. After getting the number, he thanked me and hung up.

Ten minutes later my phone rang again.

"Can you meet with the pastor and me at the house this Sunday at 10:00 a.m.?"

"No. If I'm meeting with you, it can't be at the house. Call the pastor back and ask for the meeting to be held at the church," I said.

"Okay," he replied. Within five minutes he was on the phone again, confirming that the meeting would not take place at our home but at the church.

Something about this conversation and how it was going was unusual because my husband rarely carried out my wishes without fussing. Sometimes he wouldn't fuss, he simply wouldn't do what I asked.

On the morning of Sunday, February 28, 2016, the Lord woke me up and I heard,

Pack your things.

I rolled over, sat up, and rubbed my eyes. Looking around, I surveyed my environment which, by then, was becoming familiar. *Pack your things.* I literally heard the words and realized that it was the Holy Spirit speaking to me. I argued with that still small voice, but eventually allowed the Holy Spirit to have His way. I started packing my things, but while I did, I made a mental note to park my car far enough away from the church so that Paul wouldn't see its contents if he happened to pass by. I didn't want him to prematurely discover the instructions the Holy Spirit had given me.

Waiting in my car on Unity Street in the Frankford, Philadelphia area, I saw the pastor pulling into the church's parking lot. I got out my car and walked towards Pastor Morgan. Paul got there prior to our arrival, and was leaning against a fence, diagonally across the street from the church. He started walking toward us and I slowed my pace, allowing him to catch up.

"Hi, how are you?" I asked.

"I'm not even sure," he replied.

"You alright?" he asked after a pause.

"I'm okay."

When we got to Pastor Morgan's study, he invited us to sit, and after praying, looked across his desk at Paul.

"Paul, you requested this meeting with your wife and me. What's on your mind?"

"Pastor," my husband began, "I may not be able to say it in the best words, but I hope you understand. I need forgiveness, healing, and salvation."

I remember Pastor Morgan and I both staring at Paul, at a loss for words.

"So, what does this mean and where is all of this coming from so suddenly?" I eventually asked.

What followed was a conversation that spanned more than three hours. Paul poured out his heart to Pastor Morgan and me, telling us that although his mother had raised him and his siblings in church, once he got older, he left the church. He referenced some of the things that had driven us apart like the reasons he was seldom at home. He talked about leaving work at 11:30 p.m. and hanging out with his coworkers until the wee hours of the morning instead of coming home. It floored me to hear Paul tell Pastor Morgan of all the times I would pray with him and talk to him about God with him remaining unresponsive.

During that meeting, I learned, for the first time, that Paul had won numerous awards at work for being kind and honest. He described one specific occasion on which he received a monetary gift because he had turned over to hospital management a large sum of money he had discovered while cleaning a discharged patient's room.

"Fiona doesn't know that part of me because I'm not home a lot and when I am, I don't talk to her much," Paul admitted.

The conversation continued, Paul's voice cracked, and he intermittently wiped away tears. Pastor Morgan counseled us extensively. Among the things he advised, was that we be mindful of the way in which we speak to each other. One of the things he taught us was use of the "I statement." When addressing an issue that has the potential to escalate, he taught us how to reframe our comments. For instance, instead of saying, "You didn't wash the dishes even though I asked you to," we could say, "When I noticed that you didn't wash the dishes as I requested, it made me sad."

"So, where do we go from here?" I asked at a convenient pause in the conversation.

"I want to have Bible studies and be baptized," Paul said, holding my gaze. "I want to do what you do at church."

I couldn't believe this was happening. The pastor and I exchanged surprised glances.

"Fiona," Pastor Morgan said. "From the moment I came to this church, every time you requested prayer, you asked that we pray for your husband's salvation. I guess this is it."

My heart overflowed with joy. My only words were, *Thank You, God!*

At the end of our discussion, with tears streaming down his face, Paul hugged and kissed me, reached into the backpack he was carrying, and pulled out a gift bag. He handed it to me. "Happy Birthday. You can start writing," he said.

I was taken aback at his words, *You can start writing?*

"Thank you," I responded. "I am coming home."

"You're coming home? Thank you! Thank you!" he said, smiling through the tears and hugging me.

Removing the *Happy Birthday* gift wrap, I found the leather-covered journal at which I am now looking. On the cover was the imprint "TRUST" in large letters and below that, in smaller print, the verse, "Blessed is the man who trusts in the Lord." Unzipping the journal, I saw lined pages with a bible verse at the bottom of each. I started that journal on February 28, 2016, thanking God for answering my prayers.

My husband never knew that I specifically told God I would start my book of testimonies when he gave his life to Christ. I had not mentioned a word of the arrangement the Lord and I had, but Paul handing me my 54th birthday gift and his words, *Happy Birthday, you can start writing*, confirmed for me that I should write this book and keep my promise to God. After all, He saved my husband and gave me back my marriage! I am eternally grateful and will shout it from the mountain top!

On our way out of the pastor's office, Paul made a request.

"May I see the sanctuary?"

Elated – like a kid showing off her new school – I excitedly took my *new* husband on a tour of the church at which we would worship.

Today, we serve the Lord together. Although there are still thorns in the rose bush, life is so much better, and we handle many situations differently. In the past, minor disagreements could result in us either giving each other the silent treatment for weeks at a time or exploding into bitter arguments. In most cases, I had to be the 'bigger person' so that life could get back to normal, but sometimes, even so, Paul would still not speak to me for quite a while. Today, he cannot even stomach the whiff of an argument developing between us. Our disagreements are resolved way before they ever get out of hand. While there was once a time when we couldn't have a discussion without it dissolving into a huge argument, today, it's easier to talk about the most disturbing matters, pray about them, and watch God move.

In service to the Lord, Children's Ministry is my passion and there were times when I couldn't find anyone with whom to work when visiting kids in my church's community. I remember sometimes walking the streets alone, inviting children to our church's programs, and I would pray, *Lord, I need a partner with whom to work in your vineyard,* and many times, the Lord responded: *Paul is your partner.* At the time, I couldn't see how it would happen and I doubted whether it was God speaking to me. In retrospect, I see that God had a plan to save my husband even before I saw it unfold; even before I called.

If you are praying for a loved one, *Pray on*! *Level with God*! *He has already answered!*

CHAPTER TWO

"O Lord my God, I cried out to You, And You healed me. O Lord, You brought my soul up from the grave; You have kept me alive, that I should not go down to the pit."

Psalm 30: 2 – 4

There is disagreement among Bible commentators as to whether this Psalm is a "song at the dedication of the house of David" or whether it was "A song. For the dedication of the temple. Of David." Truth be told, the fine points matter little to me; what does matter is my profound gratitude to David for taking the time to pen these verses. Irrespective of whether it was intended for the temple or his palace, he acknowledged the fact that God came through for him and delivered him. As a result, he lifted his heart in praise, honor, and glory to his God.

From the depths of my heart, I can sing as David did because I understand what he meant as I lay in a hospital bed, stricken by COVID-19 considering the very real possibility that my husband and I could die, but God came through for us! After God beat back the forces of darkness and snatched us from the jaws of death, what better words could we utter than:

"O Lord my God, I cried out to You, And You healed me. O Lord, You brought my soul up from the grave; You have kept me alive, that I should not go down to the pit."

That is exactly what God did for us.

In verses 11 and 12 David reported that God turned his *mourning into dancing; put off his sackcloth and clothed him with gladness* and informed us as to why God did that for him - so that he would continuously sing praises to Him (God) and not be silent. God did the same for my husband and me and we cannot be silent! Join with us in praising Him!

The Devil's Agenda – to Kill us . . . BUT GOD!

Thanksgiving 2021 was quickly approaching, and my family was in great expectation of celebrating the holiday. For the first time in several years two of our daughters would be home at the same time. It was cause for celebration! One of them arrived the day before the holiday, and the other, the night after the holiday. They planned to spend about 11 days with us.

Thanksgiving was great but a few days later, our older daughter, Odessa, was sick, intermittently, for a little more than a week.

On the morning of December 5, the day Gayette, our younger daughter, was leaving, I woke up feeling awful. Although I had a slight fever and was extraordinarily tired, we all rode with Gayette to the airport. Odessa had planned to leave on that day too, but her plans changed, and she decided to stay on with us for a while longer.

Gayette's flight was an early one and we were at home by 6:00 a.m. I longed for bed and went back to sleep. I awoke around 10:00 a.m. needing to use the restroom. A feeling I had never experienced engulfed me. I recall thinking, *I feel so bad, I hope I can make it back to the bed.* The next thing I knew I was lying on the floor in the hallway, with my husband holding my head up and shouting, "Odessa, call 911! Odessa, call 911!" I opened my eyes and remembered asking, "Oh, I fell?" My forehead hurt and I was bleeding a little because I had struck my head as I fell to the floor.

I was taken to Jefferson/Frankford, hospital in Frankford, Philadelphia, where I had a CT scan, an EKG, and had my vitals checked. I was then informed that I would have a 15–22 hour wait as the hospital was teeming with people who were in critical condition – many on ventilators. They further informed me that I would have to remain in the wheelchair in which I was sitting because there were no available beds. I sat in that wheelchair – my feelings going from bad to worse. I longed to lie down and after about ninety minutes I had had enough.

"If I am going to die, let me die at home, not sitting in this wheelchair. I want to go home," I said to my husband and daughter. They went to the nurses' station, and I am not sure what was discussed, but we left shortly thereafter. On returning home, I went back to bed. The next morning, I woke up feeling a tad better, but I called out from work. By evening, I had begun to feel horrible again. It's hard to describe the sensations I was experiencing.

By this time, I was entertaining the possibility that I had probably contracted COVID-19, so in addition to constantly praying and reminding God that He promised to heal our diseases (Psalm 103:3), I began to try all the homemade remedies I had heard of . . . steaming, drinking onion and honey, oregano oil, the grapefruit concoction, in addition to the vitamins that were already part of our regimen. On that Tuesday morning, I decided to return to the Jefferson/Frankford Hospital. Of course, the ER was packed, once again, and I was told that I would have to redo the CT scan and EKG as the results could change. And, of course, there was the same infernal 15-22 hour wait. I returned home.

I noticed that I had developed a cough that hurt my stomach, and as time went on, got painfully worse. Walking up the steps to our front door was tremendous work. The coughing was violent and continuous. Navigating the 13 stairs leading to my bedroom was even worse. I was forced to stop and sit two to three times when ascending and descending. Later that day I called my doctor's office and had a video conference with the nurse practitioner. She explained that because of the symptoms I was experiencing I couldn't come to the office to see the doctor. So, she prescribed medication for the cough and ordered a COVID test.

Sadly, my husband was developing the same symptoms. For the most part, he seemed well and didn't complain, but I could see that he was rapidly losing weight, had no appetite, and was coughing, though not nearly as badly as I was. He also had a video conference with his doctor. On Thursday December 9, I tested positive for COVID 19, as did my husband a few days later. Thus began the fight of our lives. I started enlisting every prayer warrior I knew to intercede on our behalf. You see, the devil may have his agenda, but God's Word reminded me that *no weapon formed against me shall prosper.* I also reflected on David's prayer in Psalm 30: 2-4 when he recounted how he cried to God, asking Him for healing. God healed him and saved his life.

Very often the Lord speaks to me through dreams. One night, while I was sick, I had two dreams in quick succession. In the one that really stuck with me, the word DIABOLICAL appeared in bold letters taking various forms: as a puzzle, dancing, flipping, darting through the air . . . Simply put, the word was just doing a number. I began asking Google in the dream: *What does diabolical mean? What does diabolical mean?* I received no response.

Later that morning my son called to check on me and he repeatedly used the word *diabolical* in reference to COVID-19. He basically said everything about COVID-19 was diabolical. I did not share my dream with him – not at that time. I Googled the word *diabolical* and learned that it had everything to do with the devil and evil. I concluded that COVID-19 was demonic and started praying against Satan and his evil plans.

On December 13, Odessa started experiencing intermittent pain in her abdomen and back. We made it through the week, but neither my husband nor I was getting any better, and Odessa was still in pain. On the morning of December 18, she decided that we should go to Urgent Care. My husband drove us there but didn't think he needed to see the doctor.

The Urgent Care doctor listened to my lungs and announced that I was in respiratory distress. He advised me to go to the ER. Thinking about the long wait I would probably have to endure, I decided against the idea. Plus, that day was one on which I woke up feeling better. On those good days, I hoped feeling better signaled the end of the sickness.

By evening, Odessa decided to go to the Penn Medicine ER to try to find out what was causing her pain. A CT scan was performed, and she was sent home as there were no notable findings.

That night, as on previous nights, sleep was a stranger. I watched the hours go by. Every shallow breath I took brought piercing pain to my stomach and sharp, shooting pain up my sides. This caused me to spend the night sitting up, groaning and coughing. Medication did not help. Eventually, I decided that on the following morning, which was Sunday, I would also go to the Penn Medicine ER.

By 5:00 a.m. on Sunday, the ER nurse called Odessa and asked her to return to have her CT scan redone. When she left for the ER, so did I. My husband offered to drive, and on our way, I tried to convince him that he should also check in. Reluctantly, he did.

At the ER, we were all separated. I got a bed on which I lay groaning and coughing, still grappling with the continuous pain. I had another CT scan and EKG and after about an hour the doctor came to my room.

"You are very sick," she said. "You have bilateral pulmonary embolism; blood clots have taken over your lungs. That is what is causing the pain. You will have to stay here for a while. You also have pneumonia and the flu."

I tried to remain calm as she quickly outlined the treatment plan which focused primarily on thinning the blood and managing the pain.

"What about my husband and daughter?" I asked.

"Your daughter is being treated. She will be discharged. Your husband is in the same position as you are. We are arranging a double room so you can be together."

That made me feel a tad better, but the devil whispered - *you both will die here together.* This was no comforting thought given the fact that we had just lost two members from one family (a mother and daughter), as well as two cousins (a husband and wife), all to COVID-19.

We were taken upstairs to the *wards*. And I say *wards* because at the last minute they decided that we shouldn't share a room because of the increased risk of medication errors since we shared the same last name. So, there we were in the hospital – a floor apart.

Things got worse before they got better.

I was in the hospital, on medication – you would think I would begin feeling better. Instead, the pain and the coughing worsened. My pain killer was administered every four hours which eased the pain about 90% but within three hours, the medication wore off and it was as if the pain was saying, *Fiona, I am here for you now.* When the pain became overwhelming, I kept calling the nurses, begging them to administer the next dose. Of course, they did not grant that request. The pain medication began to lose its effectiveness after about three hours, which meant that I would have to wait one more hour before I could have another dose and about forty-five minutes to an hour before it would take effect. The pain persisted until the medication started working. This was the drill all day and all night. Eventually, I was prescribed a stronger pain killer which worked better.

When I checked in with my husband, as usual, he assured me that he was doing well, although, by then, he was on oxygen.

On our third day in the hospital, I was weak. Every breath I took and movement I made was painful. I could hardly answer the nurse when she asked how I was doing. When she left, I cried for the second time during this entire ordeal. This time I prayed what I thought would be my final prayer.

God, I feel like this is it. If You are going to take me, please let my heart be right with You. Forgive me, cleanse me, wash me, and let me spend eternity with You. I cannot do this anymore Lord, I am tired. Please take care of my family. I give myself to You.

After praying that prayer, within my spirit I heard the Holy Spirit whisper, "Plead the Blood of Jesus. Plead the Blood of Jesus."

I am not sure why, but at the time I felt that I should plead the Blood of Jesus aloud. With some effort I eventually whispered – *the Blood of Jesus!* I said it a few times with each utterance stronger than the one before. Then that word – DIABOLICAL came forcibly to my mind. I continued praying and started cancelling the demonic forces of darkness of this disease from me, from my family, and from everyone who was sick at that time. As I was praying, I felt a presence lift from me and leave the room. I literally heard the door click like it normally would when it closes, even though I did not see it being opened. From that moment, I began to feel better, and every day was better than the day before. My husband started improving too. Our daughter was already better and had been discharged.

Eventually, I was moved into my husband's room, and was released shortly afterwards. My husband was released a day later.

Looking back at our ordeal, I now cherish life more than ever before. When people ask, "How are you doing?"

"I am thankful I can breathe," I respond. I can breathe without those sharp pains! I am even more grateful that although I may have been breathing with intense pain, I was never unable to breathe. Thank you, Lord!

I am learning daily to see *God in everything* as some say, so when the negative situations arise, I keep looking for the positive. While I was sick for more than a month, there were friends and relatives contracting COVID-19 who recovered in four or five days, and at times I wondered about that.

You see, the devil had an agenda to take us out, but God showed up! Among other things, He birthed within my spirit the need to continuously pray for others who are dealing with this disease. He gave us a wonderful testimony of His healing power and allowed my husband, my daughter, Odessa, and me to spend memorable quality time together. We do not always have to endure a test to have a testimony, but through those trials that test our faith and make us buckle, make us want to give up, or even make us give up, through God's grace and mercy, we emerge victorious and there is no greater testimony.

Thank you, God! We can breathe - without pain!

CHAPTER THREE

But I would not have you to be ignorant, brethren, concerning them which are asleep, that ye sorrow not, even as others which have no hope. For if we believe that Jesus died and rose again, even so them also which sleep in Jesus will God bring with him.

1 Thess. 4:13-14.

Millions of sermons, telling listeners that their loved ones who had died were in heaven, have brought incredible, but false comfort to many. I, too, used to believe this fallacy. I remember embracing my two sobbing children, Odessa, 13 and Whitney, nine, as we stood over their father's coffin. Then I uttered the only words I could think of to comfort them: "Don't cry, your daddy's in heaven."

I later learned that there was no truth in the statement, *Your daddy's in heaven*. Did I lie to my children, trying to bring them comfort? Yes, I did. But possibly it was an innocent lie, if such a thing exists. A lie rooted in ignorance – the result of not reading and studying the Bible for myself. And I believe this lie would be exposed if more people read and studied God's Word for themselves. Let me help you find clarity about the state of the dead from the Word of God.

What is death?

Jesus himself emphasized the fact that death is a sleep. Our loved ones who have passed on, are resting in their graves, and will do so until Christ comes again. Job 14:10 – 12 tells us, "But a man dies and is laid low; man breathes his last, and where is he? As waters fail from a lake and a river wastes away and dries up, so a man lies down and rises not again; till the heavens are no more he will not awake or be roused out of his sleep."

Jesus himself spoke about death as a sleep when he was on his way to raise Lazarus from the dead. The disciples thought that he meant literal sleep, but Jesus let them know clearly that he was speaking of Lazarus' death. John 11:11 – 14 says, "Our friend Lazarus has fallen asleep; but I am going there to wake him up." His disciples replied, "Lord, if he sleeps, he will get better." Jesus had been speaking of his death, but his disciples thought he meant natural sleep. So, then He told them plainly, "Lazarus is dead."

To make this clearer, let's go deeper:

What/who is the soul?

There are some who believe that the soul goes back to God when we die. But before thinking that way we should first clarify what – or who – the soul is. Genesis 2:7 tells us, "And the Lord God formed man of the dust of the ground and breathed into his nostrils the breath of life; and man became a living soul." This verse tells us that I am a soul, and you are a soul. No one part of us is the soul. A soul is not a separate entity apart from you or me. We are all living souls. See also: Ezekiel 18:4; Genesis 2:7; Job 27:3.

Now let's see if the application of a formula can help us understand this so-called mystery better:

Formula:
Body + breath = soul
"And the Lord God formed man of the dust of the ground and breathed into his nostrils the breath of life; and man became a living soul." Genesis 2:7.
Or
Body + breath of life in nostrils = soul Genesis 2:7

Body + spirit of God in nostrils = soul Job 27:3
Dust of ground + spirit of God (breath of life) = soul

At death, dust returns to the earth and the spirit returns to God. Ecclesiastes 12:7 says, "Then shall the dust return to the earth as it was: and the spirit shall return unto God who gave it. Therefore, it is the spirit, which is the breath of life, that returns to God.

Further, for humans to go on living in heaven or hell after death, they must possess an immortal body. First Timothy 6:14 -16 tells us that only Christ is immortal. At the resurrection, on the last day, the dead who die in Christ and those who remain without tasting death, will then "put on immortality," and go to be with the Lord forever: 1 Corinthians 15: 51 – 53.

The dead will simply sleep in their graves until Christ resurrects them at His second coming. This evidence is shown when Paul said in Acts 2:29, "Men and brethren, let me freely speak unto you of the patriarch David, that he is both dead and buried, and his sepulcher is with us unto this day." Like David, our loved ones who are asleep in their graves are awaiting the resurrection day.

Can we communicate with the dead?

Those who claim to have spoken with dead relatives are misguided and misleading. We must believe that the dead are dead, or the devil will deceive us through psychics and others who claim that they're able to communicate with the deceased. Ecclesiastes 9:5 - 6 tells us, "For the living know that they shall die: but the dead know not anything, neither have they any more a reward; for the memory of them is forgotten . . . neither have they any more a portion forever in anything that is done under the sun." See also Psalm 146:4; Isaiah 38:18.

And why would Paul tell us in 2 Corinthians 5:8 "We are confident, I say, and willing rather to be absent from the body and to be present with the Lord?" Since the dead lapse into a state of unconsciousness, Paul knew that after he died, his next conscious thought would be the resurrection, no matter the length of time between his death and Jesus' return.

Overall, the dead are asleep in their graves and will rise at the sound of God's trumpet on the day of Christ's second coming. Souls cannot go to heaven when they die because they must wait for this corrupt, mortal body to be made immortal and incorruptible, or await a resurrection to destruction. See John 5:28-29.

Where are the wicked dead, or those who die without accepting Christ?

The wicked dead are in their graves awaiting a resurrection of destruction. No soul is yet in hell because Jesus said in Matthew 25:41 that hell is prepared for the devil and his angels who will be destroyed at the end of time.

What happens to the wicked who are alive when Jesus returns?

When Jesus returns, the wicked who are alive will be destroyed and will remain dead along with the rest of the wicked until the 1000 years (the millennium) are over. See 2 Thessalonians 2:8; Jeremiah 25:13 & 33.

What happens to those who die in Christ?

The righteous dead must all wait in the grave for that time of change when Jesus comes to take us to heaven. See 1 Corinthians 15:50-55. Even King David is waiting in the grave for that day of change. Acts 2:29 & 34 says, "Men and brethren, let me freely speak unto you of the patriarch David, that he is both dead and buried, and his sepulcher is with us unto this day . . . For David is not ascended into the heavens."

David is waiting in the grave. Sampson is waiting in the grave. Solomon is waiting in the grave. Abraham, Isaac and Jacob are waiting in the grave. Adam and Eve are waiting in the grave. All the dead in Christ are waiting in the grave. But one day soon, as it says in 1 Thessalonians 4:16-17 "The Lord himself shall descend from heaven with a shout, with the voice of the archangel, and with the trump of God: and the dead in Christ shall rise first: Then we which are alive and remain shall be caught up together with them in the clouds, to meet the Lord in the air: and so shall we ever be with the Lord."

Until then, may the dead rest in peace.

24 Days

The diagnosis blew our minds! It's always someone else, not us or anyone within our circle. My husband would quip, "We never think we could make the news!"

The twenty-four hours of waiting were unbearable. Unbearable, perhaps, because I suspected the worst. My closest friend of 18 years, J, had not been doing well for several weeks. Initially, she had a flu-like symptom that seemed unshakeable. A continuous cough plagued her, she had no appetite, was constipated, and experienced what seemed like a lingering case of the common cold. Then, she began rapidly losing weight. Those stubborn pounds that for years had refused to budge, she was now swiftly shedding. Clothes that once fit snugly, now hung loosely on her frame. Finally, what appeared to be her menstrual cycle, which had stopped several years prior, suddenly returned.

"J, you should go see the doctor," I said to her on the phone one evening.

"Yes," I called today and made an appointment.

"That's good. When is it?"

"Next Thursday," she replied.

She called me about a week later with a report.

"The doctor said that everything seems okay, but he ordered some blood work, GYN checks, everything."

Less than a week later, J received the results of her blood work. Except for low hemoglobin, everything was fine. Her doctor suggested some over the counter iron pills and told her to return within two weeks for another blood test, hoping for improved iron levels.

October 29, 2018 was an ordinary Monday. J was scheduled for her second blood test. One of our church sisters, Dr. Doris, called me around 10:00 a.m. trying to locate J, who had not been feeling well, and had contacted her for a ride to the hospital. J, however, was unreachable. She was not answering her phone.

"Oh? I will try calling her, too," I said, ending the call, and trying J's number. It just kept ringing on the three attempts I made. J was someone who answered every telephone call, so when I couldn't get her, my uneasiness mounted. I was distracted, and although I tried to concentrate on my work, I kept checking my phone, hoping J would call. She didn't. An hour later Dr. Doris called to let me know that she and J were at the Einstein Hospital ER in Elkins Park, Pennsylvania. J wasn't doing well. She was experiencing shortness of breath and was in pain.

"Okay, I will be praying for her. Keep me posted." I said.

Three hours later, J called me. There were blood clots on her lung. She was admitted to hospital for further checks to determine the origin of the clots.

Despite the X-ray results, J was in high spirits that afternoon, laughing and joking with her visitors, but something about the situation made me nervous. After we left the hospital, I spoke with Dr. Doris, who held a Doctor of Nursing Practice and was a nurse practitioner.

"Fiona," she said, "I am concerned about J's situation. For the most part blood clots form after a surgical procedure or if someone has cancer."

"What are you saying, Doc?" I asked, my heartbeat quickening. "She hasn't had surgery. Are you saying J may have cancer?"

"I don't know, but we have to pray."

As I walked to my car, I was enveloped by a myriad of emotions, and tears stung my eyes. I wanted to scream.

"Devil, you are not going to do this! J shall be well!" I shouted, hitting the gas, and speeding away from the hospital. *This can't be happening!*

The area of Township Line Road, Elkins Park was lit only by the light from the sparse traffic. Easing off the gas and allowing my Honda CRV to cruise at about 30 mph, I thought about J and smiled as I recalled when we first met. There had almost been a confrontation. It was a situation that caused me to dislike her instantly, although she hadn't known it. Just a few months earlier, I had confessed why I would sometimes say to her "When I first met you, I didn't like you."

"Why is that Fiona? I never did anything to you," she would say with that seductively soft voice, and then we would both start laughing. I was long over the episode, so I didn't see the need to revisit it, but she pressed me to tell the story only a few months prior, so I did.

I was baptized and became a member of the Mizpah Seventh-day Adventist Church in Philadelphia, PA in August 2001. Less than a month after my baptism, my brother-in-law, who was the pastor there, was being transferred to another church, so the members of Mizpah organized a farewell service for him. J was one of the planners. My brother-in-law was asked to invite his family and friends, which is how my husband, and I came to be there. My husband had attended church neither before nor after my baptism, and since I had only just begun going there, none of the members, including J, knew of my affiliation with their pastor. All they knew was that I attended church with my three children.

When we arrived at the venue, we saw tables reserved for family and friends. My husband chose one of them and we sat with him. J, whom I had only seen at church a few times, approached us.

"Sweetheart, y'all can't sit here. See if you can find other seats," she said, smiling, then leaving hurriedly when someone beckoned her.

My husband got up. The children and I followed. We went to another reserved table a little farther away from the pastor's table. J approached us again with the same request. I didn't respond but looked at my husband and rolled my eyes. We moved. Again. I sat down next to him, and said,

"If she comes to us again and asks us to find other seats, I will be spending the rest of this evening in the car."

"Don't worry about it," was his response.

Although J didn't approach us again that night, I began to harbor a growing dislike of her. I would attend church and steer clear of her, but she was nice to the children and to me. Because I cannot pray sincerely when there are things in my life that I need to make right, my disdain didn't last long. At prayer time the Holy Spirit would remind me about my feelings towards her. I couldn't keep up the charade any longer, so one morning, on my knees, I came clean with the Lord. During my teenage years, there was a woman, Carolyn, at my church in Guyana, who, for no reason I could identify, I just didn't like. One morning as my best friend and I were about to enter the church compound, we saw her.

"I just can't stand her; she frets me," I said and sucked my teeth.

Yvette stopped abruptly and spun me around to face her.

"Where do you think you're going with that attitude? Not to church! You're going before a holy God, and you need to be right. Now, stand here, pray, and ask God to forgive you and help you to love Carolyn before you set your foot in His house."

Oh, that there would be more Christians like Yvette!

Yvette, who was about five years my senior, loved the Lord. She didn't play when it came to her Christianity, and she aspired to be an example to others. She made me stand there and pray aloud. It was as if God instantly answered that prayer. I walked into church smiling and never felt the same way about Carolyn. I grew to love her, and we became dear friends.

With that experience in mind, I spoke to God about J.

"Lord," I said from the depths of my heart, "you know that I don't like her. Please help me love her."

Just like He did with Carolyn, I watched the Lord instantaneously fill me with love for J. Not only did He fill me with love for her, but He filled her heart with love for me. Our friendship blossomed and we were soon inseparable. I found J to be the kind of person who touched lives. She had the gift of hospitality and people were drawn to her. Sometimes I pondered the fact that it had to be God who really drew us together. J was an extrovert who loved people while I was an introvert who welcomed the slightest opportunity to escape the crowd. Despite the differences in our personalities, the Lord knitted us together like He did Jonathan and David.

As I negotiated the tight parking space in front of my house my thoughts drifted back to J's current situation and the fact that I had just left her in a hospital bed. *This can't be happening!*

Day 1

When I visited J in the hospital she was in high spirits.

"How ya, Sis?" I asked, smiling, but only with my lips.

"I am good but pray for me. They did blood work, and I am waiting for the results."

"What do you want me to pray for?"

"For the stuff that's happening and that I get out of here quickly," she said, sipping water from the straw in the Styrofoam cup she was holding.

"Okay we can pray now," I said, taking her hand.

I cannot recall the exact prayer I offered at J's bedside that day, but we prayed and sang.

Day 2

By the end of the day, there were still no test results.

Day 3

I walked into the hospital, consumed by trepidation because I had heard from J's niece that the results weren't good.

J's brother and two other friends were at the hospital when I got there, and she was laughing and talking with her visitors. The others left the room a little later, leaving us alone.

"What did the doctors say?" I asked.

"There is a tumor in my uterus; it is cancerous and too large to be surgically removed."

It was as if I were hit with a ton of bricks. My heart sank but I stood there stoically, not daring to show any emotion. After all, this was *her* condition, and she seemed calm. I didn't understand but I chose not to disturb her peace by allowing the tears stinging my eyes to fall. I made my way to the window and brushed the tears away quickly before turning around.

"So, what do they intend to do?" I asked.

"They will try to control the blood clots. They've set up an appointment for me to see the gynecologist. I'll be discharged when my condition is stable and then I can have outpatient chemotherapy to shrink the tumor. After it's reduced, they'll operate."

"Sounds like a plan," I heard myself say, although my heart felt as if it was being ripped from my chest.

Visitors came and went, and we sang and prayed until 9:00 p.m., the end of visiting hours. I just wanted to get away from the hospital and from the people and retreat to my car. The moment I closed my car door, I bawled: "God, You can't allow this! No God, no; Lord, You have to heal J; please God, please heal her."

Later that night I shared the diagnosis with my husband.

"I can't believe this, I just can't believe this," Paul kept mumbling.

Day 4

I awoke at 4:30 a.m. and went before God. I was part of a prayer group that got together via conference call. We met routinely every day at 5:00 a.m., but sometimes, before joining, I spent time alone with God. This was one of those mornings. I poured my heart out to God on behalf of my friend who really was more than a friend to me. She was closer to me than my sisters and we were partners in ministry at our church. At that time, I was the leader of the Children's Ministries Department, and J was the wind beneath my wings, while she was ministering in the hospitality department. God carried us and she was there for me when I needed physical and spiritual support. We looked out for each other and held each other accountable. We had the kind of relationship in which each supported the other, sharing both joys and sorrows. We were partners in crime, too, oftentimes mischievously teasing someone, or getting into trouble in one way or another. Best of all, together we accomplished a lot for God.

"God," I started praying, "You said in Your Word *if I regard iniquity in my heart you will not hear me* (Ps. 66:18). Lord, I need You to hear me on behalf of my sister, so I ask You to clean me up this morning; forgive me of my failures; cleanse me from every sin; create in me a clean heart and renew a right spirit within me. Lord, You said in Your Word, call upon Me and I will answer thee and show thee great and mighty things of which you do not know (Jer.33:3). Father, cancer is nothing for You to heal, so I call upon You to show up and heal my sister! You must do something for J, Lord. Father, J needs You. You are the greatest Physician, You are our Healer, You are able, You've never lost a case, God! You heal the sick, You raised the dead, there is nothing that is too hard for You. Please God, do something for J."

While I waited, as I did in my quiet moments immediately after praying, I heard these words: "This will be a short journey." I was puzzled. *A short journey?* While praying later that morning, I heard it again, "This will be a short journey." Since I and many others were praying that God would heal J, I figured He was telling me that she would not be sick for long; He would step in and heal her in such a miraculous way that all the praise and glory would go to Him.

In addition to that word about *a short journey*, the Holy Spirit directed me to the book of Romans, chapter 8 verse 28 where I sought answers: And we know that all things work together for good to them that love God, to them who are the called according to his purpose.

He also directed my attention to verses 35 - 39: "Who shall separate us from the love of Christ? shall tribulation, or distress, or persecution, or famine, or nakedness, or peril, or sword? As it is written, for thy sake we are killed all the day long; we are accounted as sheep for the slaughter. Nay, in all these things we are more than conquerors through him that loved us. For I am persuaded, that neither death, nor life, nor angels, nor principalities, nor powers, nor things present, nor things to come, nor height, nor depth, nor any other creature, shall be able to separate us from the love of God, which is in Christ Jesus our Lord."

These scriptures encouraged me to think of and commune with God even more. I really didn't know what He was saying to me. Then I began wondering, if He would take J. Why did He direct me to scriptures which asked, *what shall separate me from His love?* Why was I reminded that neither death, nor life, nor angels, nor principalities, nor powers . . . absolutely NOTHING must separate me from Him and His love? "No, God, don't take her," I heard myself tell Him repeatedly. But the scriptures to which He directed me were asking me about what could separate me from His love. Why would He send me there? The list of questions I had was unending. Then I remembered that several months before J was hospitalized, I was plagued by images of her lying in bed, sick. I even saw her in a coffin. Those were not dreams; I'm not even sure if they were visions. They were thoughts that intermittently encroached upon my mind. When they came, I would attribute them to the devil, and would constantly rebuke them. And no, I never shared them. Not with anyone. Not even with J. Especially not with J. After her diagnosis I did begin to share them with a few people to whom I was close. Then I began to ponder another scripture: "For the Lord God is a sun and shield: the LORD will give grace and mercy and glory: no good *thing* will he withhold from them that walk uprightly." I pondered that scripture – if He was going to put J to rest, that was not a good thing, as far as I was concerned.

In the days ahead – the next 20 days, in particular – I held fast to those verses believing that God would answer my prayer, but that in whichever way He chose to answer, I had to believe that He was still God. He knew best; whatever He did was well done and nothing – absolutely nothing – would separate me from Him, even if He chose to take J. That was a harsh reality for me to face.

We are taught in God's Word that we must believe in faith that He will grant us what we ask of Him, and that He only requires faith the size of a mustard seed to work with us. That is not much faith at all. If I held a mustard seed in my hand, I would not be able to see it very well and if it fell, I wouldn't find it easily, if at all. We are also told that God knows what is best for each of us and answers our prayers according to His will. The big question was: Would I be willing to accept *His will* when He answered?

When I visited J later that day, she hadn't urinated, nor had she had a bowel movement. She still wasn't eating very much, but she was taking fluids. The doctors decided that it would be best to insert stents to help the urination process. During the surgery they discovered that the tumor was quite large and was resting on her right kidney. Because of this they couldn't insert both stents as they had planned.

Day 5

After a clinical conference on November 1, 2018, the decision was made to have a specialist join the team to try again to insert the right stent. Thankfully, the second attempt was successful We continued to pray that God would do something miraculous for J.

Day 6

While driving to the hospital I was talking to God and He said, "WRITE." *Huh? Are you telling me to write about J's journey?* I felt confirmation within my spirit.

J smiled brightly when I entered her room.

"I walked today, Fi," she said.

"Oh really? How far did you walk?"

"Only for about ten minutes; right on this floor; I used the walker."

"That's cool," I responded returning her smile.

"On my way here, the Lord told me to write, J," I said.

"If the Lord told you to write, then write, Fiona," she responded matter-of-factly.

The stents seemed to be working and J began resting comfortably. Her hospital room stayed busy. Friends and family members visited continuously. I was sometimes concerned about the much-needed rest she didn't seem to be getting, but she has always been the life of any party, sassy and witty. It was no wonder that both the young and the old flocked to her bedside. She touched everyone with whom she came into contact.

Day 7

On the first Sabbath (Saturday) that J spent in the hospital, I decided to spend the day with her instead of going to church. While packing my Bible and hymnal, I heard a text notification from my phone. The message I read made me smile:

> *November 3*
> When all else has failed, perhaps we went to the wrong one first.
> Cast your cares on the Lord and He will sustain you; He will never let the righteous fall. Psalm 55:22 NIV.

The text was from Priscilla. We were in the same boat – knocked down by J's diagnosis and still trying to wrap our minds around the inevitable. We were fighters, though, and knew that we had to get through this ordeal together.

"How ya, Sis?" I asked J when I got to her room. I put my bag on the windowsill, washed my hands, then went to her bed and kissed her forehead. She seemed relieved that I had eventually shown up.

"How was your night?" I asked.

"Not bad."

"Did you eat or drink anything?"

"A little."

It was then I noticed how badly her legs and feet were swollen.

"Did they see your legs? What are they doing about it?"

"The nurse said she'd tell the doctor," she replied.

"Well, you may not be able to attend Mizpah today but we're gonna have church up in here," I said.

She smiled.

We had hardly sung two songs before the room was besieged with family members from New York. That was it for church! The day progressed as family and friends came and went. Just before visiting hours ended, we joined hands and prayed for J as the sun set on Saturday evening and we marked the end of the Sabbath.

Day 8

From this point the journey began to feel like a roller coaster. Seven days before, J had walked into the hospital and now she was confined to a bed. Another X-ray revealed blood clots in both legs. Later that day, she underwent an emergency procedure to stop the clots from reaching her heart. Through all this mayhem, she stayed strong. That evening, before the emergency procedure, Priscilla and I had been running errands trying to get J's home ready for her return, but when we heard about the surgery, we aborted our plans and rushed back to the hospital. Shortly after we got there, the nurses began to prep her.

"Come on, walk with me," J said, signaling from her stretcher.

We accompanied her until the point at which we were not allowed to go any further.

"The procedure should take about an hour," the nurse informed us. "You may wait here until she gets back."

The waiting room was empty. Priscilla and I prayed during that hour.

J was a trooper. When we saw her next, she was being wheeled through the waiting room, her thumbs up. *She wasn't allowing anything to diminish her trust and faith in God despite what He was permitting.* Her courage strengthened our faith.

Day 9

The days felt like they were slipping away. J's discharge date kept changing. Instead of discharging her, the doctors decided to transfer her to the main hospital a few miles away. The wait for that transfer was almost an entire day, but the change significantly reduced the amount of driving I would have to do when I visited.

As I was leaving her room, J called out to me.

She motioned for me to come back.

"I want you to get two other people and pray for me. I want one of you to pray for my breathing problems and the shortness of breath; the other must pray for the tumor in my uterus and the complications in my lower stomach. The third person must pray for my legs which are continuously swollen because of the blood clots."

"You got it, J. I will gather two others and we will pray."

When I got into my car that night, as usual, the tears got the better of me, though not for long. I got on my phone and called two people whom the Lord impressed me to contact while J was giving me her instructions. I told them of J's request, and they were only too happy to be of service. When I got home, I joined that conference line at 9:30 p.m. (This was not our usual prayer line.) By the time we had finished praying, it was 12:30 a.m.

Day 10

It felt like we got bitter-sweet news. According to Doris, blood work was ordered and reviewed, and God had intervened. J's electrolytes were improving and were stable and the urine in both folies and nephrostomy had cleared up. However, she had developed hemoptysis – spitting up pieces of blood clots from her lungs, which had to be treated. Every day of J's journey was different from the day before.

Her discharge date continued to change. She seemed to be getting physically weaker every day, although her faith was getting stronger. J encouraged those who visited her, and she did not tolerate pity from anyone. She rebuked those who would break down and cry. One day, a friend she had known for many years dissolved into tears; J simply looked at her and said, smiling, "Don't mess up your face." Her friend couldn't help but laugh.

"Fiona," J said later that evening. "Thank you for being so positive. Roxanne came here today and started crying. I had to tell her, 'Girl, stop!'"

On another occasion someone said something that she wasn't having, to which she responded, "Didn't you say God's got this? So, if He's got it, He's got it!"

It's good that we're not able to read minds. Were that possible, J would have seen that I was falling apart, but somehow, God gave me the courage to put on a brave face when I visited.

Later that day, J learned that her cancer was at stage four. Family and friends continued taking those roller coaster rides with her – rides that included an ever-changing discharge date. She grew weaker and needed a blood transfusion. By then, she was not as chatty as before and her voice was softer. She was taking only a little liquid and ice and was dehydrated. Her legs remained swollen, but we continued praying.

Day 11

I joined others at the hospital. J's room was crowded. She had a biopsy that day and returned to a room teeming with friends and family. Nurses ordered excess visitors to go to the waiting area as they tried to enforce the 'two visitors at a time' rule, which didn't last long. You see, J was special in her unique way. You couldn't meet her and not be drawn to her regardless of whether you were young or old. All the children were "Auntie J's Number One." They competed for that honor.

If you mentioned in her hearing that you felt like eating a food item, she would make it or purchase it. I don't think the word, 'no' was in her vocabulary. Even the nurses quickly learned of her hospitality. They found out that she was vegetarian, and her favorite dish was barbequed tofu; she had her niece, Ann, give the nurse the recipe.

Half an hour before the end of visiting hours that evening, J looked over at me.

"Fiona, you didn't sing for me this evening," she said with such a straight face, I could feel the rebuke. I didn't even realize she had noticed that I sang and prayed with her whenever I visited.

"Okay, let's sing," I said, and began singing her favorite song:

Come on up in this room, come on up in this room
Don't you know, Jesus is my doctor,
and He writes down all of my prescriptions
Surely, He gives me all of my medicine, up in this room.
Holy Ghost, won't you come on, up in this room . . .

Every time I sang that song for her at the hospital, I thought about the times when we visited sick people at nursing homes and hospitals and sang them that song. This time the tables were turned. She was in the sick bed, calling on God to write her prescriptions and give her the medicine. It felt surreal. Like J, I wasn't known for my singing, but we both loved music and enjoyed praising God. J loved the upbeat songs and moved her body to the rhythm whenever and wherever possible.

I recall scolding her one evening while we were out shopping.

"Hey!" I said sternly, as she swayed to the pulsating beat of one of Beyoncé's melodies. "This is Walmart and that is not a gospel song!"

"Oh! Sorry!" was her only response, and she stood there with a smirk on her face.

In her hospital bed, she would move her hands and toes as we sang – the only parts of her body that she could move. Thinking about how much she enjoyed music, I remembered a video someone sent me of a toddler, getting down to music, not caring a whit about anything or anyone. When I forwarded the video to Priscilla, she texted me back, "She will grow up to be Auntie J."

Day 12

It was an incident-free day. J was stable. She chatted and drank a little soup. She updated us on who had visited her and who brought her the two tropical orchids that sat on the windowsill. She even requested coconut water and asked about the upcoming all-night prayer and fasting sessions Pricilla, and I had planned.

On my way to purchase the coconut water, I stopped at her house to check her mail and gauge how much longer it would take the workmen – friends and family - to complete the project they were doing on her house before we could start cleaning up. As I entered, I felt a sense of impending doom, and experienced an emptiness the likes of which I had never felt before. "God," I prayed with tears streaming down my face, "Please, You have to bring J back here to her home. This is where she belongs. Please God, heal her, make her well, bring her back to her house, God." Truth be told, when I walked into her house that day, I considered, with much trepidation, the possibility that she might not make it back there.

Day 13

I spoke to J by telephone early on Friday morning, before leaving for work. She sounded well, had a good night's sleep, and even had a bowel movement. That was good news indeed, so I decided to celebrate by going to the hair salon – an excursion I had put off since J got sick. My plan was to go to the salon after work and visit J later. That was not to be. By 3:00 p.m. my appointment was cancelled. I got word that the doctors discovered additional clots and J wasn't doing well. There was no way I could sit at the salon, getting my hair styled while my dearest friend was in turmoil. I rushed to her bedside and found her in pain. She remained in pain for most of my visit.

Day 14

The situation looked foreboding, but we didn't lose hope. The all-night prayer meeting Priscilla and I planned was scheduled for November 10, to be preceded by four days of prayer and fasting. I had learned that God steps in – if He chooses to – when the situation seems out of control and there's nothing man can do. After all, he stepped in when Lazarus was dead for four days! *And He was still on time!* Yes, my faith wavered somewhat during that time because knowing J's situation, only a miracle could turn things around. It was at this point that Priscilla declared we would *walk by faith and not by sight*. So, I trusted God for a miracle and prayed, "God, help my unbelief if I am not believing You enough for you to come through for J. Please God don't let my lack of faith stop You from working on J's behalf."

J's situation wasn't the only one we prayed about during the prayer vigil, although hers was the most critical. The vigil was conducted via conference call. Fifteen people were on the line. We petitioned God from 10:00 p.m. on Saturday night until 6:00 a.m. on Sunday morning. We sang and played music. Some read from the Bible; others testified of God's goodness. It was a Spirit-filled eight hours. I didn't sleep that night – didn't even take a momentary doze. I wanted God to heal J so badly, I didn't care what it cost me.

Day 15

I couldn't visit J as I spent most of that day lying in the ER of a Philadelphia hospital. During the prayer vigil, I had a heat pack at my side because every deep breath that I took was painful. My husband insisted that I go to the ER but by the end of the vigil I just wanted to hit the sack. The pain I experienced when I woke up was much worse, so I took his advice and headed to the ER where I was diagnosed with a muscle strain. Oh, how I wished this diagnosis could replace J's.

Day 16

Tuesday November 12 was Veteran's Day. It was a day off from work for me, and since one of the two appointments I had that day was cancelled, I got home earlier than I had anticipated. I had just got in and put the groceries on the table when Priscilla's name popped up on my caller ID. It was 10:30 am.

"Hi. What's up?" I asked.

"They cannot do anything more for J."

"Priscilla, you didn't say that. What do you mean?"

"They are sending her home on hospice."

"**WHAT**?? You don't mean that! No, you don't mean that!"

Tears were cascading down my cheeks. "There must be something else they can do, Priscilla! How can they just give up on her? I am heading over there; talk to you later," I disconnected the call.

I shouted for my husband who was in our basement.

"I'm heading to the hospital. They just gave up on J. They can't do that. They just can't do that!"

"Fiona, I am sorry," he said looking up at me from the bottom of the stairs. "Please drive carefully."

It was the longest drive from Castor Avenue to Tabor Road.

God, this is not happening. This is not happening, Lord. Father, please, do something for J. Please God, reverse this decision.

When I got to the hospital, I dried my tears, put a smile on my face, and walked into J's room. She was sitting up in bed, looked as if it was just another ordinary day and all was well. She obviously was at the place where she had decided, *Lord, not my will but Yours be done,* and she was prepared to trust God, whatever His decision.

Two friends were already in her room. I kissed her forehead. "I'll be back shortly," I said, before returning to join those who were outside. Her niece, Ann, who was chatting with Doris, was in tears.

"She told the doctors that if her heart stops, she doesn't want to be resuscitated." I felt like I had never heard anything more devastating and heart-rending.

When we reentered J's room, we found a team of doctors there.

"There is nothing else we can do but make her comfortable. She said she would prefer to have hospice services at home and not at a facility. We are okay with that. We would advise relatives and friends to begin spending quality time with her."

The team left shortly thereafter, and as J's niece followed them out of the room, I heard her ask:

"Based on your experience, Doctor, how long does she have?"

I didn't hear his response.

"What did the doctor say?" I asked her when she returned.

"One month," she whispered.

My body grew weak, and I felt as if my heartbeat slowed with every facet of this new development.

At J's bedside, Dr. Doris asked, "J, do you really understand what they are saying?"

Nodding, she responded, "Yes."

"And how do you feel about that?" Ann asked.

"It's not over until God says it's over," J said, her face expressionless.

"You got that right," I concurred, moving closer and grabbing her hand. "We will get through this. We have to get through this."

Dr. Doris later told me that J informed the nurses that she was tired of all the needles poking for blood tests and she wanted it to stop. So, they disconnected her IV. She was only receiving pain medication.

For the rest of that day, we chatted like everything was normal. Like it was just an ordinary day. But my stomach churned every time I thought about the fact that it was not just an ordinary day. My sister was dying. The doctors had given up on her. That news spread like wildfire, and soon J's hospital room was brimming with family and friends. Even co-workers showed up.

Day 17

I sent J's sisters in New York a group text:

> *A pleasant morning to you, my sisters. I guess you all were able to talk and decide on J's situation. Where do we go from here? Our plan is, with continuous prayer, to aggressively pursue holistic medicine, for natural healing. Do we have your permission to contact a doctor, who works with cancer patients for natural healing?*

Their answer read:

Go ahead. It's ok. Anything to help her.
Thank you, I replied.

When I visited J that evening, she looked uncomfortable and groaned intermittently.

"J, are you in pain?'

She nodded. When I checked the chart in her room, I realized that her last dose of pain medicine had been more than three hours prior. I proceeded to the nurse's station.

"Good evening. The patient in 601 is in a lot of pain. Please help her."

"Okay. I'll be there shortly."

True to her word, almost as soon as I returned to J's room the nurse showed up. Other friends and family started arriving. As we waited for her pain to subside, we began singing and praying. Before I left her that night, I explained to J that we wanted to pursue holistic treatment.

"Is it okay to go that route?" I asked.

She nodded, yes.

"Okay, we will work on that right away and tomorrow I will pick up some items at the herbal store and contact the doctor in North Carolina."

"Okay," she said. "Keep praying for me."

"Certainly, girl! Have a good night."

The others bid her good-bye and we left.

Driving to and from the hospital alone, running errands for J and trying to get her house in order made me miss her more than I can explain. Many referred to J and me as road runners. J didn't drive, so she usually rode with me or Dr. Doris. When I took trips or she needed to go somewhere, we did it together. So, sitting in my car, alone, driving without her felt weird. I missed her so much.

Day 18

J's chart had a discharge date of Thursday, November 15, 2018. Since the medical team had given up on her, we knew that the only way that date would change was if she became unstable. We undertook the task of getting her home and prepared for her arrival with a sense of urgency. Her bedroom was situated on the second floor of her three-story home, but since she was unable to walk, we adjusted her home so she could be accommodated in her dining room.

When J was initially admitted to the hospital and the doctors had planned to send her home to give the tumor time to shrink, she had given us instructions about how she wanted to be accommodated. Friends and family pitched in to help and did more than she requested. I recall that on the second day of the project, her brother-in-law showed up at the hospital.

"J, I can't understand. I left five men at your house. One on the roof, one doing the bathroom, another painting, one in the yard hauling away stuff . . . Which one of them is yours?"

Smiling, J replied, "They're all mine!" referring to her friends' husbands.

Day 19

I took the day off to assist with setting up for J's return home. While Dr. Doris and J's niece, were with her at the hospital, Priscilla, one of her brothers, two of her favorite "brothers" from the church, and I were at the house. It snowed that day. More than five inches of accumulation. The hospital gave us an ETA of 4:00 p.m. By 8:00 p.m., she still hadn't arrived. Constant checks with the hospital revealed that she was still waiting because of unplowed roads and backed up traffic. Just after 8:00 p.m. Dr. Doris told the doctors there was no way we were going to take our loved one home in those weather conditions. Plus, by that time, it was already dark. We all went home.

Before we got J home, the team of family and friends worked out a schedule that would enable her to be monitored around the clock.

We decided that she would not be left alone and would be taken care of by at least two people at any given time. This turned out to be an easy task because for most of the shifts, there were as many as five people available to look after her. She had a hospice nurse for one hour, but that wasn't every day. J, who was a certified nurse assistant, was blessed to have the support of several medical professionals from our church as well as among her friends and family. Dr. Doris led the team. I was probably one of the few people, if not the only person on the team, who didn't have a medical background. I did my share of running errands, feeding her, reading to her, singing, and praying with and for her, talking with her, and making sure she was comfortable.

Day 20

On Friday November 16, 2018, J made it home, accompanied by Priscilla, Doris, Ann, and other family members. Although she wasn't saying much by this time, she was alert and stable. When Priscilla asked her if she knew where she was, she responded,

"I am home."

That's when I remembered asking God to allow her to return to her house, the day I felt she would never return. He had answered. J was home!

I was at work but checked in with J's team. Everything seemed to be going well, so I decided to make the long overdue trip to the hair salon and didn't check in as much, especially since I had planned to be with J that weekend and every night during the next week. Halfway through my appointment, I received a call from Dr. Doris.

"Fiona, when are you getting here?"

"Probably in the next two to three hours."

"Why so long?" she asked, concern resonating in her voice.

"I have to take an uber home, then get my car and clothes because I will be there for the weekend. Why? Are you ready to leave and need me to be there before you go?"

"No, you just need to get here," Dr. Doris responded. I still didn't get it.

"Who is with you?" I asked.

"Priscilla, Ann, and a few others, but you need to come soon. Don't go home, just come,"

"Okay," I said, eventually sensing that all was not well. "I'll just go get my car and head over."

I got to J's house a little after 7:00 p.m. Several people were there, and the atmosphere was somber. Friends surrounded her bed.

Doris and Priscilla were sitting on the sofa.

"What's going on?" I asked, as I approached J's bed.

"Come, sit here, Fiona," Dr. Doris said.

I sat next to her on the edge of the sofa. "Her breathing tells us she is traveling," Dr. Doris said. She is breathing from her stomach taking pauses of about six to eight seconds between breaths."

"Do you mean she may die soon?"

"I know it's not a good sign," Dr. Doris remarked.

I went to J's bedside, held her hand and started talking to her. This was the first time that I had seen her since she left the hospital on Wednesday night. So much seemed to have changed over the course of just two days. She seemed weaker; her eyes weren't completely closed, and she no longer squeezed my hand. She was groaning much more.

"J, are you in pain?" I asked.

She shook her head slightly, no.

A hospice nurse later explained that as someone dies, his/her groaning is related to lung function and doesn't necessarily mean that the person is in pain. We also realized that we could tell whether J's groaning signaled pain simply by looking at her face. Her face was contorted when she experienced pain. Now, her face was expressionless.

J seemed to be slipping away. I let go of her hand and sat in a crumpled heap at the foot of her bed. I couldn't wrap my mind around what was happening. Friends and family kept arriving, including the young people from our church who quickly shared the news with one another. The last young person to learn of J's circumstance was away at school in Washington, D.C. She didn't even know that her Auntie J was sick. "I'm on the next train to Philly," she told the others.

Our pastor eventually showed up. Shortly afterwards, the deafening silence that shrouded the house was broken as someone began singing. Several others joined in, lifting spirits and changing the atmosphere. Around 1:00 a.m. J's breathing stabilized. We didn't lose her that night although we thought we would have.

Day 21

This was the third Sabbath that J was sick. I hadn't been to church since her diagnosis. I intended to spend that time talking, reading, singing, and praying with her. On the weekends, she had more visitors, including family and friends from out of town. By this time, we had begun the holistic treatment, but she still wasn't eating. She was still groaning and keeping her eyes opened seemed to be a struggle. Since she got sick, she took to crossing her arms over her head as she lay in bed, but now she could only lift her right arm. She struggled to lift her left arm past her chin, and eventually gave up.

Day 22

My check in with Dr. Doris via text should have given me a clue.

> *Fiona: Hi Sis, where are you?*
> *Doris: Home, under my comforter, covered from head to toe.*
> *Fiona: What's wrong? Not feeling well?*
> *Doris: I just want to be away from it all. Pray for me.*

I called in to the prayer line and requested prayer for her. What I didn't realize was that Dr. Doris, as a health care professional, already knew that J was slipping away and was trying to cope with that reality in the best way she knew how.

These were days when I fasted, prayed, and cried out to God on J's behalf. Many others joined in. Prayer line sessions focused mainly on petitioning God to turn things around for J. I asked the Lord to heal her. I knew He would move in the way that was best, but I chose to keep asking until I realized His answer. I was drawn to the story of David and Bathsheba in 2 Kings 12. After God decided to allow the child born of their adulterous liaison to die, David decided to fast and pray, beseeching God to save the child's life. His hope was that God would change His mind. He kept praying and petitioning God for what he wanted until he realized God's answer. He stopped praying only after his son died. All the signs were clear, but I was just being selfish; I wasn't ready to lose J. I was hoping that God would come through in a miraculous way.

Day 23

These days were spent making J comfortable. With the help of herbalists and the holistic doctor, we incorporated naturopathic items into her diet and regimen. These additions included sea moss, coconut water, soursop, vegetable soups, coupled with B17, frankincense, CBD oil, and spirulina.

Later that day, I received a text from Priscilla while I was purchasing curtains to enhance J's privacy as well as some other holistic items.

Hi Sis, don't pick up any other food items, just the curtains.

That gave me pause but I didn't question Priscilla. As mentioned, most of the people working with J were medical professionals and they knew and understood what I didn't.

It was Thanksgiving Eve of 2018, and we had planned to have Thanksgiving dinner at J's house. The young people from church told us that we could rest; they would cook and deliver the food. Dr. Doris was away for the holiday with her family, so another nurse practitioner, Ann, Pam, another family member, and Priscilla comprised the medical team that night. I joined them.

At 7:00 p.m. I asked Ann:

"So, what are we giving her tonight?"

"Nothing, anymore." she responded. "Only pain medication."

"What!?" I heard myself ask. "She is already weak and y'all not gonna give her anything? Not even something to drink? So, what about all this stuff we got her?"

No one answered. They just stared at me. I wasn't upset, I was saddened at the thought of J's condition. I later understood that they used their discretion to spare me some of the facts. You see, I was praying, expecting a miracle, and boldly declaring it. Even though they were praying too and wanted J to live, they understood the workings of the physical body much better than I did. I learned from Dr. Doris that J's oral intake was in decline and too much food/solids or liquids would be difficult for her to digest and could cause aspiration pneumonia.

Pam got up and went to J.

"Oh my! Her hands and feet are cold. Let's get her some gloves and socks."

Rummaging through her things, I found them. I stood at her bedside for a while, watching her as Priscilla began singing. She was breathing as she had on the previous Friday night, but her groans were subsiding.

Day 24

"It's 12:29 a.m." Priscilla announced, a little while later.

"You ladies go get some rest. I will stay up," the nurse practitioner on duty said, putting a CD into the player she had placed at J's bedside.

On the nights I stayed with J, my bed consisted of two comforters bundled on her living room floor, a mere five feet from where she lay.

During those times, I was always exhausted and fell asleep the moment I hit the floor.

"Fiona, Fiona, get up! Get up!" was the next thing I heard. Priscilla was shaking me awake.

I sat up. "What's going on?"

"Come. J is going." I got to my feet – which suddenly seemed too weak to support me – and rushed to J's bedside.

She was still.

"Go upstairs. Get her brother," Priscilla instructed.

My feet were shaking, my heart was racing, but I made it up the two flights of stairs to J's brother's room on the third floor.

I knocked on the door. He opened it immediately.

Not really sure what to say, I blurted out:

"Come. She's not doing good."

I hurried down the stairs, with her brother in tow. We got to her bedside, just in time to see Ann gently lowering her eyelids.

There was a long period of silence. Even the music stopped. The nurse practitioner said it stopped at the exact moment J drew her last breath. We all stood there looking down at her.

"Is she gone?" her brother asked.

Ann nodded, "Yes."

It was 1:30 a.m. on Thursday, November 22, 2018. Thanksgiving Day.

We stood around her bed. No one spoke. I stood at her feet. She was the picture of perfect peace.

In my mind, I replayed the words I heard on the morning I had cried out to God after learning that J had been diagnosed with cancer: *This will be a short journey . . . This will be a short journey . . .* I was thinking God meant that J would not be sick for long because He would heal her. Instead, God said, "No." *God said, "No." God said, "No." God said, "No!"* For many years, these words replaced, the initial answer I had gotten from God — *This will be a short journey.*

Eventually, I dropped heavily onto a chair, remembering Pam's remarks about J's hands and feet being cold. She had begun to die then. I had no clue. I thought she was simply cold. After all, it was late November.

Pam and Ann made some calls and family and close friends started arriving. The hospice nurse arrived and officially pronounced her dead. Though surreal, the coroner's arrival brought me back to reality. I watched them go through the protocol, eventually zipping the body bag that contained the remains of my closest friend, my sister, my partner in ministry, and in crime. Tears began to fall and have been falling ever since. We will never get accustomed to death, especially when it sneaks up on us and snatches away the ones we hold dear. Only God can heal our hearts of death's sting.

We all miss J terribly, but we know we will see her again because she died in Christ and 1 Corinthians 15:50 – 55 tells us,

> Now this I say, brethren, that flesh and blood cannot inherit the kingdom of God; neither doth corruption inherit incorruption. Behold, I shew you a mystery; We shall not all sleep, but we shall all be changed, In a moment, in the twinkling of an eye, at the last trump: for the trumpet shall sound, and the dead shall be raised incorruptible, and we shall be changed. For this corruptible must put on incorruption, and this mortal must put on immortality. So when this corruptible shall have put on incorruption, and this mortal shall have put on immortality, then shall be brought to pass the saying that is written, Death is swallowed up in victory. O death, where is thy sting? O grave, where is thy victory?

Until then, Rest in Peace, J.

PART II

My Perseverance Mode of Prayers

I switch to this mode when life takes a negative turn, creating situations that linger and plague us, causing us to question our faith.

CHAPTER FOUR

Call to me, and I will answer you, and show you great and mighty things, which you do not know.

Jeremiah 33:3

The Bible records God appearing to Jeremiah while he was confined to a dungeon. He was incarcerated because of unfavorable predictions he had made. They included the destruction of Jerusalem and the captivity of King Zedekiah. Jeremiah's fate illustrated the reality that folk may not always love and appreciate God's revelation and may be inclined to shoot the messenger. God appeared to Jeremiah while he was locked up and told him that he must call upon Him, or pray to Him, and He, God, would show him *great and mighty things.*

Call upon me and I will answer thee, indicates God's favor and lovingkindness, and shows that He was ready and willing to grant Jeremiah's desires. God's Word has not changed, neither has God changed. As the Scripture records, He is *the same yesterday, today, and forever (Heb. 13:8).* Therefore, the promise of Jeremiah 33:3 remains just as true for us today. God encourages us all to call on him! He says that when we do, He will show us *great and mighty things of which we haven't a clue;* things that are literally inaccessible or hidden.

Our circumstances do not determine when we call on God; our location does not prohibit us from calling on Him. My daughter, Odessa, was not literally shut up in a prison like Jeremiah was, but she was bound by crippling financial and legal challenges. This chapter is dedicated to the miraculous ways in which God worked things out in her favor. We acknowledged that only God could change her circumstances, so we called on Him, as did Jeremiah, realizing that despite the obstacles she faced, God was above them all.

An Immigrant's Story

It was Thursday, September 1, 2016, around 8:00 a.m. I was lying in bed, recovering from minor knee surgery. My older daughter knocked on the bedroom door. She was scrolling through her phone, smiling broadly.

"They sent the email! It says "Congratulations! You have passed your NCLEX" (National Council Licensure Examination).

Now it was my turn to reflect her broad smile and shout praises. "Hallelujah!! Thank you, Lord!! God, you are good! You did it yet again! Thank you, Lord!"

You may be wondering why I was shouting praises. Well, when you have experienced setback after setback, but then deliverance comes, when you see perseverance prayers being answered, and you know it was nobody but God who delivered you, you have no choice but to shout! Shout praises to Him!

Odessa, the eldest of my three children, had come to the end of one of her many long journeys. A fifteen-year journey at that! A journey on which, were it not for God, she would have given up long ago. A journey that brought our family to the place where all we could do was cry out to God, day and night for fifteen years. A journey that sorely tested our faith and sometimes caused it to waver. But we held on in confidence, clinging to the promise that *weeping may endure for a night, but joy comes in the morning* (Psalm 30:5). And that joy had finally come on the morning of September 1, 2016! We were praising God for what He had done, not only in helping her to pass that exam, but for all the times during those fifteen years when He was her Source. It was a journey on which He carried my daughter – one day at a time.

At Paul's invitation – he was my fiancé at the time – my three children and I had come to the United States in 2001. Odessa, my oldest, was 17, my son, Whitney was 13, and my younger daughter,

Gayette, was 9. The plan was for Paul and me to get married shortly after we all arrived, but when we got to the US, our plans didn't unfold in the way we had hoped. "Life" happened, and we had to put our marriage plans on hold for two years. Unfortunately, during that period, my children and I became undocumented immigrants.

Eventually, on July 29, 2003, my fiancé and I were married – a simple wedding at a Church in the presence of our two witnesses. A few weeks later, my husband and I walked into the immigration office to collect the forms he would need to petition for permanent residence for the children and me.

"How many of you are being filed for?" the immigration officer asked.

"Four," I answered, gasping for air, feeling as if something was about to go terribly wrong.

"Let me see your documents."

She examined the documents, placing three different piles on her right and one stack on her left. She then placed three sets of forms with the bundle of three that she had already made. She took the three sets of forms, along with the documents I handed her and gave them back to me. "Complete these and bring them back," she said.

She then took the one pile of documents that was on her left and handed it to me without any forms. "This one cannot be done now; she is over age."

I looked at her, speechless. A myriad of thoughts coursed through my mind. It was as if I were paralyzed and disappointed, all at the same time.

"He cannot file for her now. She is too old. A stepfather cannot file for a child who is over 18. You must get your permanent residence first and then apply for her. Next!"

The person behind me approached the counter before I could regain my composure. I looked at my husband. He appeared helpless. Nevertheless, he stepped closer, helped me gather the paperwork, and we walked out of the building.

My mind was in turmoil. So many thoughts tumbled around in my head: *Odessa is almost twenty. Twenty and illegal in the United*

States! That means she can't go to college, and she can't get a decent job. It might be three years before I'd obtain my permanent residence because initially, I'd be granted conditional resident status for one year. Even after filing for her upon becoming a permanent resident, her documents would not be processed immediately because she would have to be on the immigration's waiting list for several years, due to their perpetual backlog. To make matters worse, I learned that the processing of her application would not even begin before I received citizenship. *This is crazy, this cannot be happening!* But yes, it was happening. Odessa's young life was on hold!

I recall informing Odessa of what we were told at the immigration office when we returned home. "Y'all didn't know that? I knew nothing could be done for me," she smiled. Apparently, she did the homework I should have done, which made me feel guilty, foolish, and selfish. Had I done some research into the American immigration system, I would have known that a stepfather could not petition for a child who was over the age of 18 at the time of their parents' marriage.

Oh, if I could turn back the hands of time!

As I write this, I can still remember the lingering heartache, the suffocating pain, and the searing disappointment that gripped me the moment I learned there was nothing we could do for Odessa. Those feelings remained with me several years hence.

I didn't realize that this major setback would result in a walk of faith neither Odessa nor I could have anticipated or imagined. Later, we would reflect on the scripture which reminds us:

"And we know that all things work together for good to them that love God, to them who are called according to His purpose" Romans 8:28.

The wait was on, and the years went by. Slowly. Odessa had always wanted to become a nurse, but because of her immigration status, it didn't seem very likely to happen any time soon. Between odd jobs, volunteer work, babysitting, and working in a nursing home, Odessa found ways to keep herself busy. In the meantime, we kept praying that the Lord would open a door, somehow, somewhere.

May 2012: God Opened a Door!

Odessa met Heather and they became prayer partners. Heather encouraged her to go back to school and she concurred. At that time, she was taking care of a woman named Grace, so she decided that the best course of action would be to enroll at the Community College of Philadelphia (CCP) as it would allow her to continue working and attend school locally. But God began convicting her. She heard the Lord telling her that the only reason she was considering CCP was because she didn't trust Him. If she went to CCP, she wouldn't need to rely on God because she would be paying her own way through college. Odessa reasoned with God:

"God, you are right. I don't trust you to take care of me, but I need to."

At that moment, she launched out in faith, applying to various colleges. Among the ones to which she applied were Washington Adventist University in Maryland, Andrews University in Michigan, Hartland College in Virginia and Wildwood College in New Jersey. Odessa was still not a permanent resident, and, because of that, all but one of those institutions, declined her admission. God, however, had shown her favor. She was accepted to Andrews University and received a $30,000 scholarship to be disbursed over four years on the condition that she maintain a GPA of 3.5 or higher.

Although God stepped in and orchestrated her acceptance to Andrews University, Odessa still wasn't sure about going to school there. They still needed documentation, and the full cost of attending there for the first year exceeded the $30,000 scholarship. In the meantime, prayers were being offered on her behalf and by then, I was able to begin the application for her permanent residence.

Eventually, the embassy summoned Odessa and me for our interview. The immigration authorities informed us that since Odessa was over 21 when I petitioned for her, she now *stood alone*, making it impossible for her petition to be accepted. Her application for permanent residence was denied. Not wanting to admit defeat, I hired an attorney who advised us to appeal the decision. After incurring almost $10,000 in attorney's and filing fees, immigration denied her permanent residence application yet again. Odessa's final letter from them informed her that they would contact her with further action. That *further action* would have been proceedings for removal from the United States. The immigration system didn't care that Odessa's immediate family was in the United States and that this country had been her home since she was 17. By then, she was about 25. But my daughter and I continued praying.

My sister-in-law and her family were visiting us during one Christmas holiday. At morning worship, the devotional reminded us that there is nothing impossible with God. Further, it informed us that God is the God who *upturns systems*. That word – upturn – caught our attention. So, my sister-in-law and I prayed, asking God to *upturn* the United States Immigration System, so that Odessa and other young people in similar situations would be free to live ordinary lives. God is awesome! It was while we were waiting to get word from the immigration department about *when* Odessa would be removed from the United States that President Barak Obama instituted the Deferred Action for Childhood Arrival (DACA) policy via an executive branch memorandum. DACA allowed people who came to the United States prior to their sixteenth birthday to apply for this status which would afford them the opportunity to obtain a social security number and work permit, allowing them to move on with their lives. Like we prayed, God did this not only for Odessa, but for the countless other young people who were in the same boat (no pun intended). God, I praise you!

This is only one of the *mighty things* God did during this time. Remember, I told you that Odessa came to the United States when she was 17, which was enough to automatically disqualify her from even applying for this status. Applicants had to have entered the country by their 16th birthday. Regardless, I encouraged her to pray and submit the application. She did. God worked, upturning the immigration system, allowing Odessa to receive a positive response! She didn't fit the age criterion, but through divine intervention, she was granted the deferred action status. If that wasn't God, upturning systems for my daughter, tell me who else could have done that!

"God, I thank you, yet again!"

The only additional information immigration requested was proof of Odessa being enrolled in a college or university and proof of payment for college. This meant she had to choose between attending Community College of Philadelphia and Andrews University. She decided to submit her Andrews University acceptance letter to immigration, as well as her bank statement, showing the money she had saved for at least the first semester of college. Immigrants with the DACA status were unable to apply for and receive financial aid for their schooling. This meant that wherever Odessa went to school, she had to pay for everything *out of pocket*. We all know that the cost of higher education can be very expensive. But it was *on* from there! God had started her on this journey and there was no way He was going to leave her. He always finishes what He starts!

January 2013:

Odessa packed her bags and boarded a Greyhound bus for the 14-hour ride from Philadelphia, Pennsylvania to Andrews University in Berrien Springs, Michigan. She had transferred most of her money to the University, and although it wasn't enough to pay for the entire semester, it was enough to provide her with financial clearance so she could start classes. My daughter said she began this journey claiming God's promise in Deuteronomy 28:12 – she would be a lender and not a borrower, meaning she wouldn't use loans to pay for school because God told her He would take care of her, and she would not have to borrow.

Eventually, the time came for Odessa to pay off the balance for her first semester at Andrews. There was no money, and she still owed the school thirty-five hundred dollars. For me, at the time, living paycheck to paycheck was a luxury, and I had no savings. I advised Odessa to try to secure private loans.

"I really don't want to do that, Mom. God will take care of me," she insisted. Time passed and still there was no money. Eventually, she applied for a loan but needed a cosigner. I couldn't cosign because of my less than stellar credit and she didn't find anyone else to cosign, so we gave up on that option. Then God stepped in! Somebody said, *let go and let God!* We did!

When I first started attending the Seventh-day Adventist Church, I noticed that members were encouraged to share their testimonies during Wednesday night prayer meetings. Initially, I felt that I had nothing about which to testify during those times so, I prayed:

"God please do things in my life so that I will always be able to testify about you and your goodness."

That prayer was answered almost immediately and is still being answered today. Every Wednesday night as I attended prayer meeting, I would search my life to see how God had shown up and I testified about what He had done, giving Him thanks. Sometimes, while preparing for church, I thought that I had nothing out of the ordinary about which to testify, but God in His mercy showed up, often, on my way to prayer meeting, giving me something about which I could testify!

As I mentioned, I love to talk about what God does for my family and how He answers our prayers. Wednesday night services are also the time when prayer requests are made. On one Wednesday night, I petitioned the church on Odessa's behalf, to pray asking God to meet her need of thirty-five hundred dollars to clear her bill for the first semester at Andrews. The following Saturday, at church, one of the sisters, a friend of mine, handed me a signed, blank check.

"Let Odessa pay the balance due on her school fees with this. She doesn't have to pay it back." she said.

I was moved to tears and couldn't thank her enough.

"I am glad to do it," she responded.

I immediately texted Odessa:

Sister Ann gave me a blank check for you. You can pay the remainder of your balance due for this semester to Andrews.

Odessa texted back: *WOW!! How did she know? Did you ask her?*

No. On Wednesday night at prayer meeting I asked the church to pray that God supply that need and today she handed me the check.

Tell her I said thanks very much. I will call her tonight to thank her, too. WOW! God did say He will take care of me. Thank you, Lord! Odessa texted.

Well, the Lord had to step in and help Odessa academically, too. On one of my telephone check-ins with her she sounded stressed.

"What's going on, girl?" I asked.

"I'm struggling, Mom. Not only is my workload heavy, but these courses are hard, and it's essential that I pass with decent grades so I can be accepted into the nursing program and keep the university's scholarship."

"Well, you know what you must do. Nothing's too hard for God," I reminded her.

"Yeah, I know. Each day I remind myself of Philippians 4:13: "I can do all things through Christ who strengthens me," she said.

At the end of that semester, Odessa's grades consisted of four A's, an A minus and one B. She was accepted into the nursing program. That was the Lord stepping in again on her behalf! God be praised!

When Odessa returned home in May, she hoped to find a job that would help her save for school. In addition to the subsequent semester's tuition, board, and books, she needed money in advance for her clearance to the nursing program. These prerequisite costs included FBI and child abuse clearances, and CPR training. She was unable to find full-time employment and counted it a blessing when she was able to work a few hours per week at her old job.

Soon it was time for her to head back to Michigan. I'll give you the pleasure of hearing exactly what happened next from Odessa herself. The following is the rest of her story in her own words.

Odessa Recounts Her Journey
Fall 2013:

Upon examining my finances, I realized that the only money I had, which were my earnings, covered the costs of my Greyhound ticket, the nursing clearance, and the purchase of a pair of white sneakers to go with my nursing uniform. I had no money for tuition, board, or books, but I packed my suitcases and headed back to Andrews University.

Even though I had God's promise of His help, there were times when I doubted Him and miserably failed Him, but I am thankful for his goodness and mercy. There were times when I worried and wondered if I was doing the right thing. I even questioned whether people thought I was crazy. During this time, my family was also struggling financially. I knew when they could help, they did, but those times were few and far between. After all, the total cost of one year's tuition plus room and board was close to $40,000 – a cost that exceeded my mother's annual income at the time. There were times when I felt down and I believe it was the prayers of family, friends, and my church that kept me going.

Arriving at Andrews University, I didn't know what to do. I had nowhere to stay, so I decided to pay a visit to the housing coordinator for the dorms. Ms. Fayth.

When I approached Ms. Fayth, I started chit-chatting with her before getting to the real reason for my visit.

"Ms. Fayth," I eventually said, "I'm not cleared as yet."

"But you will be all right? Won't you?" she asked, looking me over.

"Yes, yes, I will be," I responded, even though at the time I had no clue as to how I was going to be all right. But I had to keep reminding myself that *God's got this*.

Ms. Fayth gave me documents to sign for my dorm room. After signing the documents, she placed them in a folder which she handed to me. On the cover of the folder there were two bolded words: "**FINISH IT.**" In my mind I began screaming. "**FINISH IT**" was the theme for the 2013-2014 school year. I felt God was telling me to

FINISH my education in spite of the money I needed but couldn't see at the moment. In awe of God and how He works, I collected my key from Ms. Fayth and set off to my dorm room. All I needed next was clearance for my classes. I made an appointment to meet with my financial advisor on that Sunday.

When I met with my financial advisor, I told him that I had no money, but I expected the bill to be paid because there were people who had promised to help me. He was skeptical and decided that he would have to discuss the matter with his director, which he did. Together, they agreed to clear me for classes because my bill for the previous semester was fully paid. However, they made it clear that before I returned to school for the 2014-2015 school year, the Fall 2013 account would have to be fully settled.

I was living this faith walk moment by moment, so I allowed myself no room for concern about 2014. The Lord had cleared me for another semester. Only God could have done it, especially since there were many students who were not cleared and were refused entry to the dorms and access to their classes. This was another praise moment for my God.

The course work and exams during this semester were even more challenging. I struggled terribly with my workload and classes. To continue in the nursing program, I needed grades of B or above, but I earned a C plus in pathophysiology, which kept me depressed for the entirety of my Christmas break. Technically, that C plus meant that I was no longer in the nursing program – a goal for which I had worked extremely hard – but I refused to accept defeat.

This grade and its potential consequences spurred me to contact the Chair and the Dean of Health Sciences, explaining to them my earnest desire to become a nurse. I never received a response to my letter and soon it was time to return to school to start the 2014 semester. By faith, I bought another Greyhound ticket and headed back to Berrien Springs. Once again, I had no money, and my previous balance wasn't paid off – the same balance I was warned needed to be paid in full before I could be accepted for the 2014 school year.

Spring 2014:

While on the bus from Philadelphia to Michigan, I received a telephone call from a faculty member at Andrews University.

"The nursing department is offering you and another student a chance to retake pathophysiology online which would allow you to remain in the nursing program for the spring of 2014," the person on the line said. She continued, "Odessa, this is a one-time only chance. It has never happened before, and it won't happen again."

I couldn't thank the bearer of this good news enough! Talk about parting my Red Sea! This was just confirmation that God had made a way for me to finish what I started even though I couldn't see with my natural eyes where the money was coming from. All that remained was for me to be financially cleared when I got there because I couldn't fathom that God would open one door and leave another closed. I was beside myself, sending up praises!

When I got to Andrews' campus, I relaxed in my dorm room. It was time to begin the process of getting financial clearance. I reluctantly went to see my new financial advisor who let me know that I had to meet with the director of financial services instead. I went to see the director, but, after I explained myself, she simply said,

"Sorry, I can't help you."

I left her office with a smile on my face but with a discouraged heart.

The next day I poured my heart out to God, tearfully telling Him, "I will not let you go unless you bless me" (Genesis 32:26). Further, I told the Lord that I was not giving up on my education that time around.* I was instructed to "**FINISH IT.**" During those times I would keep my mother updated and solicit her prayers as I knew she was also interceding for me.

When the next week went by and I still wasn't cleared, I began losing hope and became angry at God. He responded by asking me:

"Am I only worthy of praise in the times when I am good to you?" That brought me to my senses.

"God, you are God, regardless of what becomes of me," I responded. Then I became comfortable with the idea that I might not be at Andrews for the Spring 2014 semester. I began telling my friends my story, preparing them for the goodbye that I thought was imminent.

"God will work it out, girl, He is only testing your faith," some of them said.

At the back of my mind, I was confused. It didn't make sense that on one hand, God would open a door, allowing me the opportunity to retake pathophysiology and remain in the nursing program, but on the other hand, not allow me to be cleared so I could remain in school. Something was wrong with that picture. Also, it didn't make sense that He would tell me to "FINISH IT" but then not make a way for me to finish it.

By Thursday of the second week of school, my mother wrote a letter to the director of financial services and instructed me to follow up on the letter. I didn't feel like it. The director had already told me, "No." By Thursday evening, Andrews had dropped my classes and I received an email regarding cancelled registration. I knew I was on my way home. I can't even remember if I had enough faith to keep praying to or petitioning God. But thankfully, when we faint, there are others calling on Him on our behalf.

When I recall this point in time, my mother tells me that that was one of the times she really agonized with God over my situation. In 2007, I briefly attended Oakwood University in Huntsville, Alabama. I made it through the first semester, although I was unable to afford it. By the second semester, I grew tired of the constant struggle of having to find money for tuition and board. I eventually dropped out and returned to Philadelphia.

She said she remembered when I had to return from Oakwood University because of the same lack of finances and she was determined that the devil would have no victory this time around. So, she fell to her knees before God, crying out to Him, saying, "God, not another time! This is not going to happen to her again. You have got to see her through. The cattle on a thousand hills belong to You, the earth is Yours and its fullness thereof (Psalm 50:10). Odessa is nothing for You to take care of and you will take care of her. She is not coming home. She will finish school.

In week three of the semester, I decided to have another talk with the director. I prayed and asked God that she would be favorable towards me, that she wouldn't get tired of seeing me or yell at me. That day when I saw the director, she was pleasant and told me that I was welcomed to see her at any time, even if it was to say goodbye because she couldn't allow me to register unless I came up with a plan and some money.

That night, I thought about a plan and decided to start a "Go Fund Me" account. Since the director had been cordial, on the following day, I decided to stop by her office to tell her about my plan to start a "Go Fund Me" account to collect donations. She was unimpressed and still said, "No." Although she stuck to her word, within my spirit I felt that something good was about to happen.

Sometime during that week, I was playing around on the computer and went to the course site. I clicked on my courses, and they were all available online. I took that opportunity to complete some overdue course work. At this time, I was still in the dorm even though my registration had been cancelled. Nobody had asked me to leave.

Mothers don't rest when they know their children are struggling. My mother wrote another letter, this time to the dean of general studies. The dean requested a meeting with me. By this time, it was Friday of the third week of the semester. When the dean met with me, he asked me to accompany him to the office of the director of finance. I wasn't thrilled to meet with her again, but I had no choice. At the director's office, the dean laid out my situation, with which the director was familiar. After listening to the dean, the director apologetically explained that there was no way she could let me stay at Andrews with no money for tuition and board.

During this meeting, both the dean and the director started brainstorming how they could help me continue at Andrews University. When they had exhausted all the options they could think of, they told me that since I had no money, I should attend the Community College of Philadelphia or Lake Michigan College. However, during the conversation, they both realized that I was still in the dorm and registered for classes. They couldn't understand how that could have happened. I told them I did receive a cancellation notice but was playing around on the computer, saw that my classes were available, and continued taking them. As our conversation progressed, they realized that nearly $13,000 of my first semester's costs was covered by my personal earnings – money that I had saved. They found that accomplishment impressive, and the director immediately decided to clear me for school, saying that since I was able to work and save for the cost of my first semester, she would allow me to enroll, but I would have to find work and do 12-hour shifts during the summer to repay the university.

Making my way back to my dorm, I was amazed at God. I realized I serve a God who can change hearts. He is mighty like that! When He says He will do something, I can take Him at His Word because He will do it. I have discovered that I must believe Him and walk by faith - God's promises are for real. We should all learn His promises so that we can claim them. That faith journey continued, and I trusted God to bring me through. He promised!

Despite the challenging start God brought me through that semester with good grades, although there was still room for improvement. I passed pathophysiology with an A. Yay!! I finished my first year in the nursing program, for a total of two years at Andrews University, all on account of God's grace and providence.

Fall 2014: (Junior)

Well, God provided work for me over the summer. I saved approximately $4,000 for school. Actually, I earned a little more, but various expenses claimed some of it. I went to school with the $4,000, which was nowhere near enough. My balance was almost $25,000 so $4,000 was a far cry from what I needed.

So, back to the financial director I went. Ms. Angel. She said she wanted to help me but couldn't stop to talk because she was preparing to meet her boss for a committee meeting. She also mentioned that she was trying to gather as much evidence as possible to help me find favor with the committee – evidence such as my 3.55 GPA and the fact that I was able to pay $4,000.00 out of pocket.

I met with Ms. Angel the following day.

"Odessa, you need to clear your balance for the current semester. The only way I can see that happening is if you live off campus," she said.

Hmmm . . . how will this happen when I don't have a car? This just cannot happen since Andrew's University is in Berrien Springs, Michigan where there is no public transportation. "You may stay on campus in the guest room until you're able to sort things out. This is on the house," she added.

I don't even have to say this had to be God. Only God could allow a student who couldn't even afford her tuition to live like a celebrity on campus!

While in the guest room, I thought about what the financial director said and started looking for somewhere to stay. I found a room in the basement of someone's house for $285.00 per month. By Friday during that first week of school I paid another visit to Ms. Angel's office. Our plan still wasn't balancing on paper. She kept at her calculations while, at the same time, trying to contact her boss. She learned that he wouldn't be in the office that day.

"I am going to put you through. I always do this and ask for forgiveness later." Ms. Angel eventually said.

Overwhelmed and excited, I replied, "Thank you! I owe you so much!"

"You don't owe me anything! I just want you to earn that degree!"

At her words, "**FINISH IT**" popped into my head. Remember? God told me to "FINISH IT."

In talking with me, Ms. Angel realized that I was still in the guest room. And for free!

"Girl, God is on your side," she said, smiling. She then changed the conversation to students and tithing, something in which I, too, believed.

It was eventually time for me to move into the basement room, but I felt some trepidation prior to the move. I kept thinking that it was going to be a rough semester. Why? It was at least a half hour's walk from the apartment to school; public transportation wasn't available in that part of town; Michigan was mostly cold and snowy; I didn't have a computer and was trying to save for one; I would be getting home late after assignments at school; I had to find a job to keep the apartment… the list continued.

But, reading Matthew 6:24–34, God assured me that this was not only going to be a wonderful semester but an awesome school year. He had this! It was in His hands! Here is that scripture in its entirety:

> [24] No one can serve two masters; for either he will hate the one and love the other, or else he will be loyal to the one and despise the other. You cannot serve God and mammon.
>
> [25] Therefore I say to you, do not worry about your life, what you will eat or what you will drink; nor about your body, what you will put on. Is not life more than food and the body more than clothing? [26] Look at the birds of the air, for they neither sow nor reap nor gather into barns; yet your heavenly Father feeds them. Are you not of more value than they? [27] Which of you by worrying can add one cubit to his stature?
>
> [28] So why do you worry about clothing? Consider the lilies of the field, how they grow: they neither toil nor spin; [29] and yet I say to you that even Solomon in all his glory was not arrayed like one of these. [30] Now if God so clothes the grass of the field, which today is, and tomorrow is thrown into the oven, *will He* not much more *clothe* you, O you of little faith?
>
> [31] Therefore do not worry, saying, 'What shall we eat?' or 'What shall we drink?' or 'What shall we wear?' [32] For after all these things the Gentiles seek. For your heavenly Father knows that you need all these things. [33] But seek first the kingdom of God and

His righteousness, and all these things shall be added to you. ³⁴ Therefore do not worry about tomorrow, for tomorrow will worry about its own things. Sufficient for the day *is* its own trouble.

Philippians 4:19 was also a source of great encouragement for me: "But my God shall supply all your needs according to his riches in glory by Christ Jesus."

I prayed that God would help me meet great people and find favor with them. I prayed that He would help me engage in ministry activities, find a job, and earn superb grades.

God's got it! I'm on my way to "FINISHING IT!"

The Fall 2014 semester was rewarding. As I asked, God strategically placed people in my life to help me. I got rides to and from school from various friends. My classmates were especially generous to me – in addition to offering me rides, they cooked for me, lent me their computers, and made sure I was taken care of. I can give thanks and praises only to God who showed up and showed out! Further, the Lord provided a job for me. It was in custodial services at the university towers which helped cover my rent. I didn't get the grades I wanted but I did well enough to remain in the nursing program.

I was on my way to *finishing it!*

Spring 2015

It was a new semester, and I was back at Andrews. I returned with literally just a few dollars in my pocket. I had nothing extra for tuition, but that was okay. God's got it! Remember?

I paid my routine visit to Ms. Angel, the financial director.

"Odessa, you have to come up with something this time," she said. "I may have one scholarship for you if you can be classified as an honor student.

"Would you please hold the classes for me while I figure out how to get the money? I know that God wants me here at Andrews," I said, before leaving.

The following week one of my classes was dropped from my course load and I had to have it re-added. Back to Ms. Angel I went.

As she checked my information on the computer, Ms. Angel said with a mixture of compassion and sternness, "You're not even enrolled! How are you going to get the money? You don't even know."

"I am still thinking about different ways," I replied.

"Odessa, I will just award you the scholarship I mentioned for about $2,000. Girl, I can see you will get me fired." She then told me to register so I could be financially cleared.

Who did this? Who made spring semester of 2015 possible? God did! Through the help of my *assigned angel.*

This time I had no doubt that God would come through for me. My faith was growing stronger. Hebrews 11:1 reminds us that ". . . faith is the substance of things hoped for, the evidence of things not seen."

I'm thanking Jesus all the way!

Spring 2015 finally came to an end. I remained in the nursing program only because of God's goodness. That school year I was able to work and continue studying. I needed to do a course during the summer and wondered how I was going to pay the $535 it cost. My tax return from the job the Lord provided for me, covered that expense.

To God be the glory!

Fall 2015

My final year of school! The Lord allowed me to receive a scholarship to cover the semester's expenses even before I left Philadelphia. However, Ms. Angel requested that I pay the outstanding $2,000 needed to cover my old expenses. I was forced to revisit the loan option but once again couldn't find anyone to co-sign for me. I even tried to get a loan from my summer job, but never heard back from my supervisor.

On September 1, 2015, I paid Ms. Angel a visit because on September 2, classes would be dropped, registration would end, and I needed to be at clinicals that day. When I arrived at the office at 2:00 p.m., I was told to return at 3:30 p.m. but at 3:09 p.m., I received an automated message on my phone stating that a payment plan had been set up for me. That meant I was cleared!

I confirmed via computer that there was, indeed, a check mark at the financial plan link on my account. That was my angel again, being used by God. I was now cleared, and God did it all by Himself!

Day by day I learned to lean on God. My Father, my Provider, my Protector. He is continuously blessing me although I don't deserve it. To God be praise and glory and dominion and power, forever and ever!

Fall 2015 finally ended. God did it again! I was the first student to work in the skills lab that semester. I had the option of not cleaning toilets on holidays and my beloved friend, Jalisa, got me a ticket to Florida for Thanksgiving.

That semester I had great teachers like Mrs. Kuhn and Mrs. Plott. My learning experience was enjoyable, and I got great grades too.

Spring 2016!

Spring 2016 had come! This was my final semester!

God told me to "FINISH IT" at the beginning of my faith walk through university, and that's exactly what I was doing. My final routine visit (hopefully) to the financial director went like this:

"How much longer do *we* have?"

"It's my final semester," I replied.

"Wow! God has brought *us* this far!"

I was cleared again. The director was glad to know that I was in my last semester. Who wouldn't be glad? This angel's assignment wasn't easy. That semester I trusted God to pay my entire balance - $36,252.75. Won't He do it? Yes, He will! Andrews University deserved to be paid in full, or whatever God saw fit to do. It was all in His hands. I was making room for God to do a new thing in my life. I was also praying that I would pass the HESI (Health Education Systems Incorporated) and NCLEX on my first attempts.

I noticed that God always provided just enough for me which taught me to totally depend on Him.

Spring 2016 was the roughest semester. I had tons of assignments to complete, while still preparing for the comprehensive HESI exam – all while working. There was a lot of drama in our department because of this exam, and I failed it on my first attempt. I had to retake it, but I am sending up the praises anyway!

Something else happened that semester. I was inducted into Sigma Theta Tau International (STTI), the second largest nursing organization in the world with approximately 135,000 active members. That was unexpected, and God made it happen. And as if God had not showed off enough on my behalf, a vacancy arose at Kettering Hospital in Ohio. I applied and was offered the RN position after interviewing. I later realized that this job was an answer to my prayers that God would help me pay off my balance that was due to Andrews University. God finishes everything He starts. He did not end this journey before providing me with a job and making it possible for me to settle my balance with Andrews University, the institution to which I will be eternally grateful. God told me to "FINISH IT" and He finished it, too!

Eventually it was graduation weekend! It was amazing!

All the hard times paid off – the tears, the uncertainties, those nerve wracking trips to the financial director's office, the burdensome journey to financial clearance, the long tedious hours traveling from Philadelphia to Berrien Springs and back, endless, and challenging assignments – all culminated in those steps, walking to the podium at Andrews University, and collecting my degree: Bachelor of Science in Nursing!

I was also elated that at my pinning ceremony, I was presented with the *Image of Nursing* award, a distinction bestowed on the student who the professors believe exemplifies nursing. What a delightful surprise!

Only by God's grace did I pass the HESI on my second attempt. I also had to retake the Kaplan Readiness Exam. I rejoiced because these exams were requisite for graduating.

Then it was time to study for the NCLEX and complete paperwork for Ohio licensure. Financial concerns were once again front and center. I also needed money to renew my Deferred Action immigration status.

September 2016

Up to this point, God had answered all my prayers related to my education. I finally did the NCLEX on August 30, 2016. After completing 75 of the **265** questions the computer shut off – my test had ended, which meant that I either performed well or poorly. I left the room feeling at least 90% certain that I passed. Two days later I received an email from the Ohio Board of Nursing which confirmed my suspicions – I had passed!

On September 1, 2016, I officially became a registered nurse in the state of Ohio - Odessa Lawrence, BSN, RN.

Remember that I mentioned needing money for the renewal of my Deferred Status? Well, I didn't even have to ask – Rhonda, a family friend, and my stepfather provided the much-needed funds. I am entirely grateful for their contributions.

Now I am on to the next chapter of my life, and I am very excited to see where God takes me.

Yes, it was indeed a journey of faith.

Prior to Odessa launching out on her educational journey I had a dream one night. I saw her sitting on a low stool or bench with a very large textbook balanced on her knees. It looked like a nursing textbook. She was studying, surrounded by lights which were very bright. When I awoke, I couldn't get the lights that illuminated her presence out of my mind. I reasoned that the lights in the dream meant that God was in charge and was ready to do something great on her behalf. Remembering that dream throughout her walk gave me the courage to keep believing that God had got this for her, but I must admit that there were times when my faith wavered.

Shortly after that dream, Odessa left for Andrews University. Oftentimes, as I watched her pack her bags and leave for school, usually without money, I felt helpless. All I could do was stay on my knees for this situation. Jeremiah 33:3 became my source of comfort: "Call to me, and I will answer you, and show you great and mighty things, which you do not know." We saw God do those mighty things as He promised. During those times I came to realize that God didn't need my help because everything I tried to do never worked out. But Odessa was always able to complete every semester. I also noticed that when I stepped out of His way, that was when He worked for her. God doesn't need our help.

There were times when people made sarcastic remarks. Even family members tried to dampen her spirits…but God! However, there were also people who supported her. I recall a New Year's Eve church service during which she testified that she would be on her way to school a few days later. She confessed that she didn't know what would happen and what God would do because she had no money, but God had to do something. A sister later said to me,

"God will see her through. She has the faith and that's all that matters to Him. He works for young people when they exercise their faith in Him."

That sister's words came to fruition, and I will be forever grateful for her encouragement. Further, we proved that God always finishes what He starts. Unlike many of us who are buried under the burden of student loans, Odessa was able, through God's providence, to eliminate her balance at Andrews University within four years of graduating. What a mighty God!

Reflecting on Odessa's journey, I can only wonder: *who was the next assignment God placed in her angel's charge at Andrews the next school year?* I am also thankful for angels who accept their assignments and do their jobs to the best of their ability.

Keep praying and launch out! Remember, faith without works is dead!

CHAPTER FIVE

*"And you will seek Me and find Me,
when you search for Me with all your heart."*

Jeremiah 29:13

Did you know that there are over 3,000 promises in the Bible that God made to us and that He expects us to claim them? Second Corinthians 1:20 tells us "For all the promises of God in Him *are* Yes, and in Him Amen, to the glory of God through us." Before I share this testimony, I am alerting you to the fact that I will be using the Bible as my source. Having studied in the legal field, I was trained to always have a source with which to support my facts. Opinion carries no weight. It is the same with God's Word; when we tell people about God, we must be able to support our facts with His Word. I know I cannot please everyone and not everyone believes in the Bible, however, I find it necessary to use the Word of God and allow it to speak for itself. I like being able to go to God's Word for my answers, so, bear with me.

I have a question. What is the heart? Well, the Word of God tells us as a man thinks in his heart so is he (Proverbs 23:7). So, the heart is the mind, and we know this to be true because thoughts originate from the mind. And what does it mean to search for God with all your heart? This includes, but is not limited to, filling your mind with God by talking to Him through prayer, studying His Word, working for Him, meditating on Him, and surrounding yourself with like-minded Christians.

There are times when life's challenges bring us to a place where we realize our only hope is in God and we need Him. That's when He tells us that we will look for Him and we will find Him when we search for Him diligently.

God is our provider and sustainer, and in finding Him, we are more equipped to face life's challenges. Matthew 6:33 tells us, "But *s*eek ye first the kingdom of God and his righteousness; and all these things shall be added unto you." Many can testify of living this scripture because they have put God first in their lives and have experienced this promise.

For the most part, those who choose to follow Christ are part of a congregation but finding the right church home is challenging because congregations are such diverse groups. There was a time in my life when I was searching for God. I was trying to find Him by seeking for His true church. How do we decide which is the true church? I needed God's help in finding the truth and the right church in which to worship. In this testimony I will share how He came through for me.

The Day He Blessed and Made Holy

My relaxed mode of prayer may sometimes be short, but it's earnest. I grew up in the Pentecostal church. I loved it and am very glad for that foundation. At age 12, I felt the need to walk with God and give my life to Him, which I did, although I didn't always stay on the straight and narrow. Many of you may be familiar with Sunday School – I remember two men of God, Pastor Clark and Brother King. They used to gather all the kids from my street and have Sunday School. A few of the children from other areas also participated. The Sunday School was held on the cement base of a wooden house that was perched on high pillars. At the beginning, I was one of the most talkative and disruptive students in the class, but gradually, upon hearing about Jesus and how He loved me, I learned to love Him. Pastor Clark shepherded a church a few miles from our home and when I was baptized, I started attending the big church (as we called it).

I continued in the Pentecostal faith until I was about 40 years old at which time I moved to the United States. Once I migrated, I connected with my then fiancé's family. Most of them were members of the Seventh-day Adventist Church. One of the distinguishing features of Seventh-day Adventists is that they worship on Saturdays. While growing up, I remember referring to them as *seven devils*. My fiancé's brother, Pastor John, was the first to invite me to church. I couldn't see myself going to church on Saturdays. For the most part, Sunday is the day of worship, worldwide, isn't it? But I accepted his invitation and visited his church on a few Wednesday nights for prayer meeting and Bible study. I did not, however, attend on Saturdays.

In the meantime, I was praying and asking God to help me find a Pentecostal church. I began exploring Olney, my new north

Philadelphia neighborhood, looking for a church to call my own. I did locate a few but was never motivated to visit.

One Saturday morning it was *raining cats and dogs*. Because of the challenges of the week, my mood reflected the weather – dark, lonely, cloudy, and dismal. When I am in that space, it's so easy for me to curl up in bed. So that's exactly what I did. But I felt like I was drowning in despair. I remembered Pastor John's church and immediately yearned to be in the house of God. Without a second thought, I got up, got dressed, and went to church. By the time I arrived, the service was about half-way through. As soon as I walked in and took my seat, a woman, whom I later came to know as Sister T, smiled at me. As I had got there late, I didn't enjoy the service very much, but afterwards Sister T introduced me to a few other ladies and asked one of them to give me a ride home. This act of kindness and friendliness made me feel better and I looked forward to returning to the Mizpah Seventh-day Adventist Church the following week.

"We're going to church tomorrow," I said to my three children on the following Friday afternoon.

"Which church?" my son, then 13, asked.

"John's church."

"On a Saturday?" My older daughter, then 17, asked, frowning.

"Yep! And we will be on time. We will leave here around 10:00. The service starts at 11:00."

Nobody said anything else, and they prepared their clothes for church the following day.

In contrast to the rainy Saturday the week prior, it was a lovely, sunny morning when we boarded the bus at Olney Avenue and headed to Germantown in the northwestern section of Philadelphia. Church was about to begin when we got there. Smiling ushers welcomed us and we were led inside. Within a few moments of our getting there, the platform participants, including Pastor John and the elders, took their places. My eyes locked with John's, and he nodded approvingly.

The congregation began to sing. Certainly, the style was different from the upbeat music to which I was accustomed in the Pentecostal church, but following in the hymnal, I sang along.

"It's time for our Affirmation of Faith," the elder who was leading out said. "It can be found in the Bible, Exodus 20:8-11, or at the back of your bulletin." He paused for a moment, waiting for those who needed to find it in their Bibles. Then the congregation started repeating what they called their *Affirmation of Faith*. I followed along in my Bible. By the time that scripture was read halfway, I was stunned. I was reading something in the Bible that I couldn't ever remember hearing or seeing before! It was as if those words came alive on the page. The congregation completed the reading and moved on to other parts of the service. I cannot tell now what they did next because I couldn't stop reading Exodus 20:8-11. I read and re-read the passage:

> [8] Remember the Sabbath day, to keep it holy. [9] Six days you shall labor and do all your work, [10] but the seventh day is the Sabbath of the Lord your God. In it you shall do no work: you, nor your son, nor your daughter, nor your male servant, nor your female servant, nor your cattle, nor your stranger who is within your gates. [11] For in six days the Lord made the heavens and the earth, the sea, and all that is in them, and rested the seventh day. Therefore the Lord blessed the Sabbath day and hallowed it.

I was oblivious to my surroundings. I read those words over and over. And the more I read them, the clearer they became. But more questions began crowding my mind too – questions like:

Have I ever seen this before? Did the Pentecostal church ever teach me about the Sabbath? Isn't this a part of God's Ten Commandments? If I do not keep the Sabbath, am I keeping only nine of God's commandments? Aren't we supposed to keep all ten of the commandments? How do they know Saturday is the seventh day of the week? Which day of the week is the seventh day? . . . I was confused. I couldn't wait for church to end so I could get home to read my Bible and do some research. In the meantime, I started counting the days of the week on my fingers, trying to determine whether the Sabbath day was Saturday as these Adventist people were claiming, or whether it was Sunday as other Christians believe. *Who is right? Who is wrong?*

I thought about the calendar that we all know so well and began counting on my fingers, trying to figure out which was the seventh day of the week. *The calendar starts the week on Sunday, right? So, Sunday should be the first day of the week.* It took me a few times counting, but there it was – Saturday is the seventh day of the week. Saturday is the day the Lord blessed and sanctified and told us in the fourth commandment to *remember and keep it holy.*

Mercy! I felt betrayed. Had I been observing the wrong day as the Sabbath for almost forty years of my life? Was I keeping only nine of God's commandments and not ten? Doesn't James 2:10 tells us: For whosoever shall keep the whole law, and yet offend in one point, he is guilty of all? My mind was in turmoil. Thinking back to my days in the Pentecostal church, I recall attending regularly and faithfully, but I couldn't remember reading my Bible with the same diligence. I was one of those Christians who looked to the Pastor for spiritual guidance but never really relied on God for myself. I remember reading the Bible on my own, yes, but studying it to understand what God was really saying to me – I didn't do that. Many times, I would listen to the pastor preach, go home, and put my Bible away until the next time I went to church. *Possibly that's why I missed something so important. Was there anything else I was missing?*

Church was barely over before I gathered my children and headed home. In the privacy of my bedroom, I opened God's Word, the Bible, but before reading, prayed:

"Lord, please show me clearly what you are saying in your Word. I need to know the correct day of worship and I need you to tell me which church I should make my home." That day I began reading the Bible from the Book of Genesis. Back then, I didn't know much about how to study but I read slowly, read passages several times, pondered scriptures, and continued in that fashion for about a week.

The Lord urges us to trust Him, and we can always take Him at his Word. Jeremiah 29:13 tells us: "And you will seek Me and find Me, when you search for Me with all your heart."

All through the Bible reading, I continuously prayed, asking God to reveal His will to me. God answered my prayer when I got to Exodus chapter 16.

Exodus 16 records the story of the children of Israel after they had recently left Egypt and were in the wilderness on their way to the Promised Land. In the wilderness, they became hungry and grumbled against Moses and Aaron, saying, . . "It would have been better if the Lord had killed us in the land of Egypt. There we had meat to eat and all the food we wanted. But you have brought us into this desert to starve us to death" (NCV). God heard the complaints of the children of Israel and told Moses to tell them that He would cause food to fall from the sky like rain. Further, the Lord instructed Moses to let them know that they must go out every day and gather enough food for that day, but on the sixth day of the week (Friday) they should gather twice as much as they gathered on the other days. The Lord revealed to Moses that He was doing this because He wanted to prove the people to see if they would do what He said or not.

> "Then said the Lord unto Moses, Behold, I will rain bread from heaven for you; and the people shall go out and gather a certain rate every day, that I may prove them, whether they will walk in my law, or no." Exodus 16:4.

Moses also instructed the people as the Lord told him:

". . . Don't keep any of it to eat the next day" Ex. 16:19 (NCV). However, some of the people didn't listen and they gathered more than their share of the food/manna. What remained overnight became full of worms and stank. This made Moses angry because the people didn't listen to his instructions from the Lord.

Then it was the sixth day – Friday – and as the people were instructed, they gathered twice as much food because Moses had said to them: ". . . This is what the LORD commanded, because tomorrow is the Sabbath, the LORD's holy day of rest. Bake what you want to bake, and boil what you want to boil today. Save the rest of the food until tomorrow morning" ". . .You should gather the food for six days, but the seventh day is a Sabbath day. On that day there will not be any food on the ground" Ex. 16:22-23 (NCV).

Well of course, knowing mankind, some of the Israelites didn't listen and they went out on the seventh day to gather food. Believe it or not. They found none! Of course, the Lord wasn't pleased with His children's disobedience. This is what the Lord said to Moses because of Israel's noncompliance: ". . . How long will you people refuse to obey my commands and teachings? Look, the Lord has made the Sabbath a day of rest for you. So, on the sixth day He will give you enough food for two days, but on the seventh day each of you must stay where you are. Do not go anywhere. So, the people rested on the seventh day" Ex. 16:28-30, (NCV).

After reading this chapter a few times, I had my answer. Within the Ten Commandments, the Lord gave us instructions about the day on which we should worship, and He took time out to show us how He wanted it done in Exodus chapter 16. He, Himself, provided manna for the Israelites for six days of the week, but on the seventh day He provided nothing because that is the day He ordered us to remember, rest, and keep holy. He blessed that day and sanctified it. I needed to hear nothing else.

Almost 40 years later, just before Moses died, and shortly before Israel crossed the Jordan River into the Promised Land of Canaan, Moses repeated God's commandments (God's Law) to the people. In that address, Moses reminded the people of God's intended purpose for their experiences in the wilderness. In Deuteronomy 8:1-3, Moses stated:

> Every commandment that I am commanding you today you shall be careful to do, so that you may live and multiply, and go in and possess the land which the Lord swore [to give] to your fathers. And you shall remember [always] all the ways

which the Lord your God has led you these forty years in the wilderness, so that He might humble you and test you, to know what was in your heart (mind), whether you would keep His commandments or not. He humbled you and allowed you to be hungry and fed you with manna, [a substance] which you did not know, nor did your fathers know, so that He might make you understand [by personal experience] that man does not live by bread alone, but man lives by every *word* that proceeds out of the mouth of the Lord" (AMP).

After this personal revelation I had to make a decision – a decision upon which my salvation hinged, because God's Word tells us in Luke 12: 46-47, that if we know the Master's will and don't do it, we shall be beaten with many stripes. Also, those who do not know His will and commit acts worthy of stripes, shall also be beaten, but with fewer stripes (the latter is because ignorance of the law is not an excuse for wrong deeds [sin]). Furthermore, during a person's life, he or she would have had an opportunity to hear God's Word and to decide. This decision is important because the Word also tells us when we come upon new truth, we must act on it. Ultimately, we'll be held accountable for disobeying the truth revealed to us. Psalm 95:7-9 states: "For he is our God; and we are the people of his pasture, and the sheep of his hand. Today if ye will hear his voice, harden not your heart, as in the provocation, and as in the day of temptation in the wilderness: when your fathers tempted me, proved me, and saw my work."

James 4:7 also states: "So any person who knows what is right to do but does not do it, to him it is sin" (AMP).

Shortly afterwards, my children and I started studying the bible with bible workers from the church and we were baptized in August 2001. Since I had found this truth, I felt it was my duty to make my Pentecostal friends and family aware of what I had learned because Ezekiel 3:20 tells us: "Again, when a righteous man turns from his righteousness and commits iniquity, and I lay a stumbling block before him, he shall die; because you did not give him warning, he shall die in his sin, and his righteousness which he has done shall not be remembered; but his blood I will require at your hand." Also, Ezekiel 33:8 charges me to do something: "When I say to the wicked, 'O wicked *man,* you shall surely die!' and you do not speak to warn the wicked from his way, that wicked *man* shall die in his iniquity; but his blood I will require at your hand."

Beginning to spread this news, I was shocked that some of my Christian friends and family knew about the Sabbath and even acknowledged that Saturday was the Sabbath.

"So, why don't you worship on the Sabbath day as the Lord commands us?" I asked a few.

"Everybody worships on Sunday."

"Everybody does it."

"It's tradition."

"That is Old Testament laws; the Sabbath was done away with at the arrival of Jesus."

"I don't want to be different from everyone else."

Those were some of the excuses people offered in defense of their decision to continue worshipping on Sunday even when the Bible clearly spells out the bona fide day of worship. I found it appalling because the fourth commandment is in the middle of the ten, and God never changed the commandments. Further, Christ is our example and those who believe that the Sabbath was only related to the Old Testament and that it was done away with, will discover that there are countless scriptures in the New Testament which tell of Jesus's custom while He walked this earth: "So He came to Nazareth, where He had been brought up. And as His custom was, He went into the synagogue on the Sabbath day, and stood up to read" (Luke 4:16); "Then they went into Capernaum, and immediately on the Sabbath He entered the synagogue and taught (Mark 1:21); "And when the Sabbath had come, He began to teach in the synagogue" (Mark 6:2); "Now He was teaching in one of the synagogues on the Sabbath . . ." (Luke 13:10); "And he reasoned in the synagogue every Sabbath, and persuaded both Jews and Greeks" (Acts 18:4).

Jesus also set the example for His disciples and when we search the Scriptures, we find them doing the same: "Now when they had passed through Amphipolis and Apollonia, they came to Thessalonica, where there was a synagogue of the Jews. Then Paul, as his custom was, went in to them, and for three Sabbaths reasoned with them from the Scriptures . . ." (Acts 17:1-2).

Eventually, I concluded that if I claimed to be a follower of Christ, I had to do what Christ said regardless of what anyone else did. Even if I had to be different, I would stand for God's Word and dare to be different like Daniel did.

A few years later, our church was appointed an interim pastor when our pastor retired. Coming with new ideas, he made some changes. Change is good sometimes, but one of the changes he instituted was the removal of the Affirmation of Faith from the Sabbath liturgy. When I became aware of the change, I approached the interim pastor:

"Pastor," I said, "I notice that we are no longer repeating the Affirmation of Faith."

"That is true," he responded, "I am trying to do things differently around here."

"I see, and I do understand," I responded, "But may I share with you why that removal concerns me?"

"Sure. Why not?" he said.

I began sharing my testimony with Mizpah's interim pastor about how God changed my life as a result of reading the Affirmation of Faith from the Bible on the second Saturday I visited. "I was a Pentecostal Christian, prior to becoming an Adventist, and I held strongly to what I believed, but seeing God's instructions directly from His Word, I couldn't keep going to church on Sundays. "Pastor, you know," I continued, "We Adventists know the Affirmation of Faith by heart, and nobody can take that from us, but when someone walks into our church on Sabbath (Saturday mornings), what will they hear or see that will cause them to differentiate us from the Sunday worshipers? Had the Affirmation of Faith been removed prior to my visit to Mizpah SDA Church, I wouldn't have left here knowing why you worship when you do, instead of the Pentecostal Christians who worship on Sundays. Pastor, I think you should reinstate the Affirmation of Faith," I concluded.

"We will see," he responded, nonchalantly.

I do not know if he ever gave what I said a second thought but what I do know is that the Affirmation of Faith was omitted from our worship services for the three years he served as interim pastor.

Some people knew how I felt about the removal of the Affirmation of Faith from our worship services. I was not at church one Sabbath after our new pastor was installed.

A dear friend of mine who has since passed made it her duty to call me on the following day.

"Guess what?" she asked.

"What?"

The Affirmation of Faith was reinstated in our worship service as of yesterday.

"Yes! Thank you, Lord!" I responded.

I pray that more of our churches will stop viewing the Affirmation of Faith as just another ritual in our services but consider it as God's Word and a message for the visitors walking into our churches, wondering why it is that we worship on Saturdays, instead of on Sundays. Do we ever wonder why the Lord started the fourth commandment with the word, "REMEMBER?" He knew that even His people would treat it lightly and forget about it.

When I was a young girl, our home was located on a street in Agricola, East Bank Demerara, in Guyana. At the top of that street was a church and the people worshipped on Saturdays. I remember walking by that church many Saturdays, asking myself, *why do they do this?* Why did they go to church on Saturdays when most others, including my family, went to church on Sundays? More than 40 years later, after becoming an Adventist Christian, the Lord afforded me the opportunity to visit that Adventist church in Guyana, sit in its pews, and reminisce about my childhood, walking past that church and having questions. I testified in that church about my journey. The people marveled. A few (though much older) were still there.

Are you one of those Christians who knows that we should worship God on Sabbath, put every secular thing aside, and spend that day with Him, yet because of tradition you refuse to act on that knowledge? And when I say we should put everything aside, I do not mean we should refuse to do good on the Sabbath day. In many instances in the Bible, we see Jesus making His stop at the synagogue on Sabbath, then hitting the streets, working for His Father, including preaching the Word, teaching about God, and healing the sick. Are you one of those Christians who believes that the Sabbath is Old Testament stuff and was done away with? I have listed many scriptures in this chapter. Even though God winks at our ignorance, we will be held accountable for truth revealed to us on which we took no action.

You may ask Him this question today. Lord, what day did you set aside as being holy that I should keep holy, too? He'll answer. Try Him.

CHAPTER SIX

***Now faith is the substance of things hoped for,
the evidence of things not seen.***

Heb. 11:1

What is faith, really? Hebrews 11:1 tells us in expansive language, it is the *substance of things hoped for, the evidence of things not seen.* What does that mean? BibleRef.com defines faith in layman's terms. "True, godly faith is defined as trust, relying on God when looking to the future, and obeying even when we don't fully understand all details." Trust + Obedience = FAITH! We see faith in action when we trust what we hear, and we put those directives into action. Further, Romans 10:17 tells us that *faith comes by hearing, and hearing by the word of God.*

    Joseph, a popular Bible character, was Abraham's great-grandson. He exercised faith by instructing his brothers that when the Lord delivered the Hebrew nation from Egypt, his bones were to be carried to the Promised Land. (Gen. 50:22-26 KJV). Now, what did Joseph know of Canaan, the land God promised to his forefathers? Joseph wasn't even born during that time. However, Genesis chapter 17 records a story of God making a covenant with Abram. Among other promises that God made to Abram, was that He would multiply his seed greatly; He was going to make him exceedingly fruitful, causing kings to come out of his progeny. Thus, God changed his name from Abram to Abraham, which means "father of many nations." He also promised to give him and his descendants the land of Canaan. At that time, Israel did not yet exist.

Joseph knew of the Promised Land because back then, parents were instructed by God to teach whatever He shared with them to their children (Deut. 4:9; Deut. 6:7; Deut. 11:9; Gen. 18:9; Ps. 78: 3-8, etc.). This instruction of passing on God's Word to children and grandchildren is still a noble and worthwhile practice. Joseph, upon hearing these stories and promises from his parents and grandparents, took them to heart, believed them, remembered them, and *hoped* for them.

The instructions he gave to his family about his bones when he was about to die at the age of 110 is one of the reasons, we know that Joseph believed and acted on what he was taught as a child.

Let us break down this verse: *Now faith is the substance of things hoped for,* . . .Despite how long it took, Joseph believed with faith and confidence that God would do what He said He would do. He told them he would die and God would *surely* visit them and bring them out of the land of Egypt and take them into the land which He promised to his great-grandfather, Abraham (Gen. 50:24–26).

. . . *the evidence of things not seen* – While he was giving his final instructions concerning his bones, Joseph acted on what he believed, although he did not experience it during his lifetime. What *FAITH*! Joseph did not live to see the children of Israel go into bondage or be delivered, but he knew that day would come. He looked towards that day and he prepared for it. No wonder Joseph's directions are written in the book of Hebrews in the faith hall of fame: "*By faith Joseph, when he died, made mention of the departing of the children of Israel; and gave commandment concerning his bones.*" (Heb. 11:22).

Is there something for which you need greater faith? Does it seem impossible? Allow your faith to rise in God. In this chapter, I will show you how I allowed my faith to rise in God, took Him at His Word, and launched out.

Faith in Action!

I earned money cleaning homes when I first came to the United States in 2001. In addition to cleaning, I worked as a part-time clerk for a small manufacturer's representative. After almost five years, in 2006 I landed my third job. I was employed as a temporary data entry operator with one of the largest law firms in the northeastern United States. Not having a college degree at the time, the data entry operator position was about the highest level at which I could work in the corporate world. I wasn't satisfied, so I decided to go back to school. I was 44 years old. After completing my associate's degree in paralegal studies, I became a permanent employee and was promoted to case assistant. I continued my education and earned a bachelor's degree in paralegal studies.

Still working as a case assistant four years later, I eventually became bored and wanted more challenging work. I started praying about this situation and began yearning to be employed with the federal government. During those days I scoured the usajobs.gov website. I applied for every position for which I was qualified. After almost two years of trying to get work with the federal government, I received a call from the Internal Revenue Service (IRS).

This appeared to be my breakthrough, albeit precariously, because I was offered a temporary assignment, with a tenure of about six months. This meant that I would be leaving a permanent job with full benefits to accept a temporary job with limited or no benefits. Questions plagued me. Would the Lord take me from permanent employment to a temporary job, and for only six months? This felt like going backwards, but I knew what I had to do – pray for guidance. And I did.

I don't remember having this much difficulty to make up my mind about anything before or since. This was a complex decision since we were a family of six and our family's size had already outgrown my husband's remuneration. *What would I do after the six months were up? What if the IRS terminated me before the six-month period ended? Would I find a job quickly after my job ended?* The battle over whether I should stay in the corporate world or move forward with the federal government raged within me.

I kept praying. Then one day while reading my Bible, I came upon Hebrews 11, the faith chapter. It mentioned many things people of old did because of their faith in God:

> By faith Abel offered unto God a more excellent sacrifice than Cain . . . By faith Enoch was translated that he should not see death . . . By faith Noah, being warned of God of things not seen as yet, moved with fear, prepared an ark to the saving of his house . . . By faith Abraham, when he was tried, offered up Isaac . . . By faith Isaac blessed Jacob and Esau concerning things to come . . . By faith Jacob, when he was a dying, blessed both the sons of Joseph; and worshipped, leaning upon the top of his staff. By faith Joseph, when he died, made mention of the departing of the children of Israel; and gave commandment concerning his bones . . .

One morning, I called my mother and described my predicament. She began rehearsing parts of Hebrews 11 – "By faith," she said, "Abraham did this and by faith Noah did that…by faith Jacob did the other. You ever read those scriptures?" Listening to her, I smiled. It was time to launch out in faith.

The process of becoming a federal employee took what seemed like forever. Even after three group interviews, I still wasn't sure I had the job, so I couldn't make my current employer aware of my intention to resign. Eventually, the federal agency notified me that I was selected for the job – three business days prior to the start date, making it impossible to tender my two weeks' notice of resignation. After receiving the job confirmation, awkwardly, I walked into my supervisor's office.

"Elizabeth, I am sorry," I began. "I have some not so good news."

"What happened?" she asked, turning away from her computer and facing me, concern etched in her voice.

"A while now I applied for a federal job. The process was lengthy and uncertain, so I couldn't give my notice to resign. I just received a call that I must start on Monday. I am sorry for any inconvenience this may cause."

"Oh, that's not bad news. We would be sorry to see you go, but it's life. Congratulations!" She smiled.

I thanked her and we discussed exit procedures.

It was my first federal job and I was elated! But the reminder that it wouldn't last very long lingered in the back of my mind, so I continued job hunting, constantly searching the federal job site. By this time, I was in the first year of my master's program and keeping up with a full-time job, family, school and church activities weighed heavily on me.

Less than three months after starting this new job, the agency decided they no longer needed our services, so about 25 of us were furloughed. I tried braving the situation, reminding God that He okayed the move, but there were anxious moments. I was forced to constantly remind myself of Philippians 4:6 which tells us: "Be *careful* for nothing; but in everything by prayer and supplication with thanksgiving let your requests be *made known unto God.*"

I was laid off the IRS job for about four weeks when I was called back for an additional three weeks. It was then time to file for unemployment. I was embarrassed to file the claim because a portion of those funds would come from my corporate employment. That meant my previous employers would know that after I resigned from their job to accept a position with the federal government, I was unemployed after less than four months.

What I didn't realize until afterwards is that God, who sees the end from the beginning, knew exactly what I needed. God knew that my master's program would demand more time, energy, and study than I had bargained for. I became overwhelmed with assignments, research, and studies. It was as if college was full-time! There was no time for anything else during those courses. That chapter in my life showed me that God was looking out for me the whole time. He knew I couldn't handle a full-time job as well as graduate studies. In His wisdom, He allowed me to give up my permanent job, cushioned me with a part-time job for a few months, then gently removed that too. And He did it just for me. Being at home and receiving unemployment meant that the Lord removed job stress from my life, allowing me to attend college, study, and find time for family.

I was unemployed for almost nine months. No bill was late, no debt collector called, and we had food and even occasional entertainment. Right after those two stressful quarters of the school year, God opened another door with the federal government. I am now at my fourth federal agency for a total of 12 years. That's how kind God is!

Hebrews 11:1 reminds us that *Faith is the substance of things hoped for, the evidence of things not seen.* I trusted and relied on God for specific employment which I couldn't see in the making. With His help, I obeyed Him and accepted the position even when I didn't know what would happen when that temporary assignment ended. Looking back, I saw God relieving me of my job so I could study effectively, then blessing me with federal job after federal job. I never saw what God had in store, but I prayed, trusted Him, and launched out. Trust + Obedience = FAITH! Similarly, Joseph believed God's promise to his forefathers. He launched out in faith and commanded his brethren to take his bones with them to the Promised Land when God delivered them from Egypt. And that day of deliverance came for the Israelites.

That day can come for you today! Trust Him and allow your faith to rise in Him!

PART III

My Relaxed Mode of Prayers

*Here I share testimonies set when life's seas were calm.
There were no fierce trials and when situations arose sometimes
God stepped in and answered before I even prayed.*

CHAPTER SEVEN

***He is the one you praise; He is your God,
who performed for you those great and
awesome wonders you saw with your own eyes.***

Deuteronomy. 10:21

Sometimes, when people talk about miracles, they refer only to Bible stories such as when the Lord, through Moses, parted the Red Sea and the children of Israel walked through. Or when Shadrach, Meshach, and Abednego were delivered from the fiery furnace, and Daniel survived his night in the lions' den. We serve the same God who performed all those miracles back then, and because He is the same and He is unchangeable, He continues to perform miracles today. If we are to really examine it, we would notice that life consists of everyday miracles. For instance, not one of us is able to wake ourselves up from sleep. What about the unseen forces with the agenda to kill us? Are we able to build hedges of protection around ourselves? No, we cannot. Hence, God is still the object of our praise because of His goodness and mercy towards us and because of all that He has done – and still does – for us. He is the same God, and whatever He did before, He can do again and again, and yet again. He shows Himself miraculous in what may appear to be the little things as well as the unfathomable situations.

Deuteronomy 10:21 tells us, "He is the one you praise," which means God is the object of our praise. He has given us manifold, bountiful reasons to praise Him. "He is your God, who performed for you those great and awesome wonders you saw with your own eyes."

People who witnessed God's miraculous hand experienced awesome wonder, fear, and sometimes, even dread. After all, we are not dealing with finite man like ourselves; we are talking about God! The One who parted the Red Sea, and fed 5,000 people with five barley loaves and two fishes. The One who raised the dead, healed the sick, and spoke peace to the storm. The list is never-ending of what our miracle-working God has done and still does. Hebrews 13:8 says, "Jesus Christ the same yesterday, and today, and forever." I am thankful that God still works miracles among His people, and many can testify to this fact. You, too, may be able to testify – if you search hard enough and recall those things you knew you couldn't accomplish on your own – that *it had to be God!* Try trusting Him for your miracle today!

Shelter in a Storm

It was summer of 2011. I remember this well because I was still in grad school studying for my Master's in Public Policy. After sitting behind a mound of textbooks, reading for almost six hours, my body felt stiff, and I needed to stretch. Getting up and putting on my sneakers, I told my husband that I was going for a walk around our neighborhood in the northeast section of Philadelphia. It was about 5:00 PM; outside it was sunny and about 80 degrees. Turning the corner of Castor Avenue onto Luzerne Street, a gentle breeze rustled my hair. I noticed carefree children playing outside and light traffic going by.

About 15 minutes into my walk, the breeze became stronger, the sun was suddenly hidden by clouds, and the air felt dusty. I made a right onto Lycoming Street heading towards home; a gust of wind lifted the dust high into the air. I increased my pace, with the goal of making it home as quickly as possible. Coming upon a grocery store about halfway down the block, I contemplated taking shelter there, but reasoned that I should keep going and just walk faster. I immediately increased my pace, and at one point, started running. By the time I got to the end of the block, the wind was gusting so badly that the dust in the air was almost blinding. I kept running, barely paying attention to the fact that there was no one in sight. By the time I got to the end of the next block, the wind, which felt like it was blowing at about 65 mph, was threatening to knock me over. I couldn't maintain my balance and it was almost impossible to see what was in front of me for the dust everywhere. It was time to seek cover!

Please God, I quickly prayed. *Help me to find shelter.*

I turned the corner, and my intention was to knock on the door of the first house I came upon. Fortunately, a woman wearing white was standing behind a white picket fence at the first house I saw.

"Please, please Ma'am, may I come in until the storm is over?" I asked, shading my eyes because of the dust. I could even feel it in my mouth.

"Yes, sure," she said, smiling, leading me to the open door. Just inside the door, sat another woman who was also dressed in white.

"This is my mom," she said.

"Hi," the woman said, flashing a smile and motioning me to a chair.

"Hi, thank you," I replied, taking a seat.

I remember seeing a television, but it wasn't on, and I cannot recall if there were any other furnishings besides the chairs in which we sat. We exchanged polite, but spare comments regarding what appeared to be a sudden storm. The weather event, itself, didn't last very long – perhaps 10 minutes, at most. As the wind subsided, the woman who had invited me in, opened the door and peered outside. Looking back at me, she smiled.

"It's over," she said.

Thanking them both for rescuing me, I left. Outside, it seemed dusty, but dry, and the wind had ceased. Making my way home, I wiped my sandy face and arms, and dusted my clothes.

"Did y'all realize there was a storm out there not long ago?" I asked my husband and daughter when I finally made it home.

"I heard a lot of wind, but I didn't look out," my husband replied.

"I didn't hear anything," my daughter added.

I began to wonder if I was crazy. "I will have to watch the news tonight," I said.

"Something weird happened out there just now and I need to know what it was."

When I tuned in to the Fox 29, 6:00 PM News that evening, the news anchor confirmed that a sudden dust storm had swept through northeast Philadelphia that afternoon.

About two weeks later, I went for one of my sporadic neighborhood walks, intending to stop by the house that served as my haven during the dust storm. I wanted to express my appreciation, once again, to my rescuers. After turning right on Lycoming Street, I walked past the grocery store, proceeded down the next block, and made a right on the first cross street, just as I had done on the day of the dust storm, but the street appeared unfamiliar. There was no white picket fence to greet me as there had been when I turned the corner that day. *Am I on the wrong street?* Retracing my steps, I began visualizing what I did two weeks prior. I confirmed that I was, indeed, on the right street **but the house with the white picket fence was not there!** The houses on that block, like many others, were only accessible from the sidewalk by steps. In contrast, there were no steps leading from the sidewalk to the yard of the house where I had sought shelter. There was a white picket fence and a few feet of pavement that led to the front door, but there were absolutely no steps.

Beginning to doubt myself, I walked up and down Lycoming for about three blocks, turning onto every cross street, looking for the house with the white picket fence, and no steps. There was none! I clearly remember that there were no steps leading from the sidewalk to the front door of the house that had sheltered me. I had walked straight off the sidewalk into the front yard, and then into the house. Now, all the houses I was looking at on every block were designed to be accessed from the sidewalk only by steps, and none of those houses had a white picket fence. This experience unnerved me, although I was clear in my mind that I had seen that house and gone inside. I just couldn't understand it. My once intermittent neighborhood walks became regular because I was determined to find the house with the white picket fence that had been my haven. For several weeks I searched that neighborhood tirelessly, but never found the house. On a few occasions, I even made my husband drive me around several blocks in close proximity to the grocery store, hoping to find the house, but I never did. Eventually, I gave up the search, but I never doubted my experience, and it remains vivid in my mind's eye.

In 2016, I began chronicling my testimonies, so I asked the Lord to help me remember all the experiences I had had with Him. At that time, He reminded me of this literal *shelter in the time of storm* incident. Before I started writing, I thought about making one more attempt to find the elusive house with the white picket fence, but while I was driving around the area, the Holy Spirit convicted me:

Fiona, why won't you trust me? I prepared a shelter for you during that dust storm and here you are, doubting me. When the streets were desolate and the door to every house was locked because of the storm, you saw a woman dressed in white, standing at a white picket fence. What would she be doing there during the storm if she was just a woman? Why would her door be opened during a dust storm when every other door was closed? Why would another woman be sitting at the open door also dressed in white? Fiona, you need to know and believe that I am The Shelter in the time of storm, and I prepared that refuge for you.

I didn't need to hear anything else. I never searched for that house again, but instead, held firmly to the experience God had afforded me.

I cannot remember stopping to thank God for His deliverance during that entire ordeal. For months afterwards, I was so consumed with finding the house with the white picket fence that I didn't realize God had prepared a temporary refuge, which I can now say was literally placed there by His own hand. But I thank God that He is not like me. Even when I don't deserve it, He continuously blesses me, and He knows what I need even before I ask (Isaiah 65:24). Now I think to myself, that had I realized what was playing out, I would have taken notes. Mercy! God, I thank you!!

CHAPTER EIGHT

__Give, and it shall be given unto you; good measure, pressed down, and shaken together, and running over, shall men give into your bosom. For with the same measure that you use it shall be measured to you again.__

Luke 6:38

Are you a generous person? Have you ever given until it hurt? If you have a lot of mangoes, someone asks for one, and you give it, how does that make you feel? On the other hand, if you have only one mango, and your younger brother asks you for that mango, and you give it to him, then you are left without. Do you feel any differently from the way you did in the former scenario? I have learned that when I give from my scarcity, or I give my last, that's when I have really given! With that kind of generosity comes an indescribable fulfillment that could only be from God.

God's Word tells us we must give to others. Notice, we are expected to be proactive. We must be the first to do the honors - 'give.' Many times, we give and forget all about it, but God remembers. He then steps in and blesses, and His blessings may not always come in dollars and cents. They may come in many other ways, including good health, protection, favor… the list goes on.

Firstly, God's Word tells us that after we give, we will receive. Secondly, not only will we receive, but it will be in good measure – this measuring cup will not be half full; it will be to capacity. Thirdly, after our cup is filled to the brim, it will be pressed down, allowing it to hold even more. Fourthly, God is still not satisfied with the amount He has given to you, so, He presses down what is in the cup, still attempting to make room for more. Even that is not enough, so fifthly, our Lord allows the cup to run over!

Now, notice the Word says ". . . For with the same measure that you use it shall be measured to you again." So, if we are stingy and mean, that is the measure we will receive. If we are generous, God will be more than generous with us. Of course, we must remember that we are never to give just so that we can receive. We must also bear in mind that our generosity may not always be repaid by the person to whom we give. Things don't necessarily work out that way. In my life, I have found that, for the most part, the people to whom I often say, "Thank you" may not be recipients of my assistance when they are in need. The Lord supplies their need through other means. Let me show you how God did exponential multiplication on my behalf after I took a small leap of faith.

$2.00 Multiplied More Than 100 Times

Being a single parent with three children to feed, house, and clothe is not easy. Sometimes it takes a miracle like the one I'm about to describe, where God stepped in just for me.

Those were hard times. I was living in Barbados, West Indies, my second marriage had just ended, and I was struggling with my three children. Because there wasn't much money for food, everything else was less important. My older children's dad decided he didn't have to support them and my younger daughter's father, showing up for our divorce hearing, wearing the most raggedy clothes, and boots he could find, told the judge that all the child support he could afford was $40.00 per week.

One Sunday evening, my children and I walked a little over a mile to church. I was down to my last two dollars and pay day was a week away. I had planned to use those two dollars to purchase sugar on our way home, for the children's tea.

Because we walked to church, we arrived late. Choruses had already been sung and the offering was about to be collected. I hadn't planned to give an offering because I had no money to spare.

"Tonight, I want to challenge your faith," the pastor said while the children and I settled into our seats. "Whatever money you place in the offering plate tonight," he continued, "trust the Lord to multiply it 100 times."

Huh? I only have $2.00 and I need it to buy sugar.

I focused on the ushers as they made their way down the aisle. *I really cannot put my last $2.00 in that offering plate.*

The ushers were about two pews from where I sat. I quickly reached into my pocketbook and pulled out the $2.00 bill. By then the usher on my side of the aisle was standing beside my pew. Without thinking any more about it, I leaned past my son, and placed the money into the offering plate. "Lord, please bless this and multiply it like the pastor said," I prayed.

The service ended and soon we were on our long walk home. I went past the corner store because I had given the sugar money as offering.

The next day, less than 24 hours later, my sister called from Guyana.

"Fiona, I have a message for you from William (my two older children's dad). He wants to let you know that he sent you $100.00 U.S. for the children by Western Union and that he plans to send that amount every month from now on. He said the exchange rate should be two Barbados dollars to one U.S. dollar, making it $200.00 per month."

I was awestruck. William, who behaved like he had no financial obligation to his children, was honoring his parental responsibilities after almost ten years.

"Fiona, are you still there?" my sister asked.

"Oh yes, girl, I am here. Just sort of shocked."

"Yes, I know. Mom and I were also very surprised when he told us. But I am glad. It is time he does something for his kids," she added.

"Girl, I shouldn't be shocked though."

"Why?" she asked.

"Well only last night I was at church and the pastor challenged us to give an offering and trust the Lord to multiply what we give one hundred times. I gave two dollars and today the Lord has multiplied it one hundred times by sending me $200.00 through William. The best part is that William promises to send that $200.00 every month!"

"WOW!" my sister, responded.

Honoring his obligations to his children appeared to be the turning point in William's life. When he made that pledge, I received $200.00 via Western Union every month to help take care of the children's needs. The payments continued until four years later when we got word that William was hospitalized. He died shortly afterwards. After his death I stopped receiving the payments which started the day after a prayer and an act of faith in giving God all I had. God is faithful and we can trust Him to be generous, regardless of the circumstance.

Are you trusting Him? If you aren't, start today. Launch out in faith. You will not regret it!

CHAPTER NINE

Before they call, I will answer;
while they are still speaking, I will hear.

Isaiah 65:24

God is all-knowing, omniscient. He anticipates our desires even before we ask Him about them, hence Isaiah 65:24 starts by stating: "Before they call, I will answer…" At times, He doesn't even wait for us to ask; He supplies our needs. Sometimes we may even be unaware of some needs until much later, but God in His mercy, knows what the future holds and shows up as that present help.

The verse continues, ". . . while they are still speaking, I will hear." Imagine – He knows what we are about to ask for! We haven't even asked yet, or finished asking, and God steps in and makes provision for us. In Daniel 9, verses 20-22, Daniel testifies to this fact. While he was still praying, God sent Gabriel to grant Daniel's request.

While they were in prison, Paul and Silas prayed and sang praises unto God, according to Acts 16:25-34. Scripture does not record them asking God to send an earthquake—but the Lord did! That earthquake shook the foundations of the prison, opening the doors and breaking their chains. When the prison guard realized there was an earthquake that freed the prisoners, he was about to kill himself, afraid of what the authorities would do to him, had the prisoners escaped. Paul, realizing the guard was about to take his own life, shouted to him, "Do thyself no harm: for we are all here." As a result of this miracle, the guard accepted Jesus as his Savior.

God's promise to hear us and answer before we call should encourage us to keep communicating with Him. We must keep asking Him boldly, albeit humbly, and He will step in and take over on our behalf. Here, I am about to testify of God knowing what I would need and answering before I even asked.

Turn the Doorknob!

It was one of those days when everything that could have gone wrong did go wrong. Although I hadn't rested well the night before, the day started ordinarily, and I set out on my way to work. Once I got there, however, it was as if I couldn't do anything right. I made numerous mistakes, which caused my supervisor to yell at me several times. The harder I tried to concentrate on what I was doing, the more mistakes I made. Twice I left my boss's office, sat at my desk, and blinked away built-up tears. Eventually, it was 3:30 p.m., the time I usually left work on Fridays.

A blast of arctic air assaulted me as I burst through the doors of the Curtis Center – the building in which I worked, reminding me of the severe cold snap the state was experiencing. Hurrying down Seventh Street, I pulled my scarf tighter. Turning onto Chestnut Street, I hastily descended the subway stairs after about fifty yards, wanting desperately to get away from it all – fatigue, a bad day at work, the cold…everything, and everyone. Forty-five minutes later, I was almost home when it dawned on me – I didn't have my keys. I couldn't remember picking them up from the table that morning. *God, I hope I am wrong.*

Walking briskly towards my house from the train station, I rummaged through my pocketbook, hoping I was mistaken. When I got to my front door, I literally emptied the contents of my bag. The keys were not there. Tears slowly cascaded down my cheeks, and my frostbitten fingers began to ache. *What should I do? I wish I had known this before I left work; I could've gone to Paul's job and gotten his keys. Now I'll have to take the train all the way downtown and then to West Philadelphia. No, this is not happening!*

By this time, the tears were streaming. All I wanted to do was enter the sanctity of my home, curl up in my bed, and lock the cold world out.

Should I go to my friend's? I can take an Uber to her house. If I call Paul, I would be standing outside for too long before he gets here . . .

Bracing myself against the outside wall, I wiped away tears. I didn't want to go to anyone else's house. I just wanted to be in **my** home, in **my** bed.

At that moment, I heard a voice say, "Turn the knob."

Amidst tears I blinked and looked at the doorknob. "Turn the knob," the voice repeated.

I reached out and turned the doorknob. The door opened! Yes, the door opened!! Cautiously, I stepped inside, looking around from the doorway. Everything was in place. By that time, I was bawling. Why? I was in the house; that was what I longed for, right? Yes, but I was in the house even though I had no keys. I was supposed to be outside, either making my way to my friend's house in an Uber or to my husband's job. But I was in the house with no keys. Pulling my phone from my bag, I dialed my husband's number. He answered on almost the first ring.

"I forgot my keys! I forgot my keys!" I cried into the phone.

"What? Stop crying. I will leave work right away and open the door for you—stop crying," he said.

"No, you don't have to come," I responded.

"What do you mean, I don't have to come?"

"I got in the house. I am inside."

There was silence on the other end of the line. Eventually when he spoke again, he sounded puzzled.

"How did you get into the house?"

"I turned the knob and the door opened."

"What?" he asked.

"Yes." I just turned the knob and the door opened.

"Fiona," he said, sounding even more serious, "I did not leave that door unlocked."

"Well, I don't know what happened but what I know is that I needed to get in and a voice said to me, "Turn the knob." I did, and the door opened."

"You just turned the knob and the door opened?"

"Yes," I responded.

"Something is not right because I locked the door. Is everything in the house okay?"

"Yes, it seems so."

"So why are you still crying? Stop crying."

I guess I was crying from joy, surprise, relief, everything. Pulling myself together, I dried my tears. My husband was still on the phone, silent.

"I don't know, but I did not leave the door unlocked. I'll see you later," he eventually said.

I really don't know what happened and I will not even question it, but that verse from God's Word came to me:

Before they call, I will answer; while they are still speaking, I will hear. Isaiah 65:24. While I was still crying, He intervened!

I reasoned that God knew I had had a rough enough day and couldn't deal with another challenge, so He stepped in. I don't know how and what He did, but if He made a way for the children of Israel through the Red Sea, what is an insignificant door for Him to open? I praise you, Lord! I thank you, Lord!

Is there a situation in your life with which you need help? Is there something in the future about which you are concerned? He already knows about it! He will answer!

CHAPTER TEN

"Ask and it shall be given unto you . . ."

Matt. 7:7

What a simple command. It needs no overthinking. If you are like me, you may sometimes find yourself overthinking and making an issue out of a simple situation. Jesus Himself tells us in Matthew 7:7 that if we need something, we should simply ask Him in prayer. That includes our physical, material, spiritual, emotional, and/or financial needs. It ranges from our most basic need for food or shelter, to more complex requests such as curing a disease, or granting us wisdom and knowledge. God is God and the Bible tells us in Psalm 50:10, "For every beast of the forest is mine, and the cattle upon a thousand hills." Psalm 24:1 reminds us that, "The earth is the Lord's, and the fulness thereof; the world, and they that dwell therein." God's Word is telling us beyond the shadow of any doubt that everything belongs to God and if we need anything, we must simply ask Him through prayer. Further, we are told in Matthew 7:11 that "If we then being evil, know how to give good gifts to our children, how much more will our Father who is in heaven give good things to those who ask Him?" Our prayer can be one word, such as, *Help!* or a phrase – *God, help me!* A sentence, *Lord, I need you every hour, or* a paragraph, or even pages long. Whatever we need, God tells us to ask Him, and He will give it to us.

Now, does that mean, then, that we can ask for anything in the world that we want, and we will get it? Well, it does matter what we ask for and how we ask for it, for the Bible also says in 1 John 5:14, *If we ask anything according to His will, he hears us.* So, when we ask of God, we must be sure we are asking *according to His will.* It's been said that "Faith and doubt cannot mix." *But let him ask in faith, nothing wavering. For he that wavereth is like a wave of the sea driven with the wind and tossed. For let not that man think that he shall receive anything of the Lord* (James 1:6-7). Further, when we ask anything of God, we must remember that God is God, and He knows what is best for us. When we ask and He answers, He does so in our best interest.

In the following chapter, I describe how I needed God's help in finding something I lost. I petitioned Him, and He helped me find it!

Hidden From Their 'Eyes'

Queen's Park, Barbados was brimming with people on that sunny Sunday afternoon. We were on our way to the Singing Christmas Tree Concert at The People's Cathedral. I stopped with my mom and children to take some photos but holding the Kodak camera and my wallet at the same time was awkward. I set my wallet down on a bench so that I could take the pictures.

Sometime later, we strolled towards the cathedral, which was a fifteen-minute walk from the park. As we joined the line, my daughter handed me the tickets which were purchased before my mother's decision to visit us for the holidays. This meant that I didn't have a ticket for her. My plan was to purchase one at the door. We joined the long line of energetic people – men, women, happy children dressed in Christmas colors. I looked around, extending my hand to my son who looked at me blankly.

"What do you want, Mom?" He asked, confused.

"My purse! Did I give it to one of you?"

Four pairs of surprised, worried eyes stared at me. "No," they chorused.

"What? Did I leave it in the park? Oh noooo!"

I looked down at the only thing I carried in my hand – the camera.

"Shucks! That means I left it in the park!" I was bewildered and developed an instant headache. Apart from $80.00, my wallet contained my identification and bank cards, and a few miscellaneous receipts.

"Mom, take my ticket and go in with the children. I will race back to the park and see if I find my wallet."

"So many people are in that park, girl, I don't think you will find it," my mother replied.

"I'm praying. Be back soon," I said, hurrying away.

"Please God, help me find my wallet. Hide it from eyes that might want to keep it," I prayed. That fifteen-minute walk back to the park seemed to take forever.

On entering the park, I began looking around, praying, and retracing my steps to where we took the pictures. The nearby bench was vacant. I stood there, my heart pounding, hoping I would see the wallet somewhere. Children were playing and adults were casually strolling along while others sat watching their children. The purse was nowhere in sight. With drooped shoulders, I walked away.

When I returned to the cathedral, I realized that I had no money to purchase a ticket. I had given mine to my mother. Peering in at the door, I could see that the auditorium was dark. Although lit by Christmas lights, it was hard to recognize where my family sat.

"Grandma bought a ticket for you," I heard my son say behind me.

"Oh great!" I said, taking the ticket and giving it to the smiling usher at the door.

"I was waiting over there for you. Let us go in. I know where they're sitting," he said.

"I'm so glad y'all thought about that."

My son carefully wound his way through the auditorium's semi darkness to where the others were seated, while I followed closely behind.

"Did you find it?" My mother asked as soon as I sat down beside her.

"No," I said shaking my head.

"I'm not surprised. There were too many people in the park."

I was at the Singing Christmas Tree Concert. Everyone around me seemed jolly, but losing my wallet saddened me. I remembered the prayer I offered up on my way to find it and wondered if I should pray again. I didn't. However, my mood quickly changed when the band started playing and the melodious choir joined in, capturing my attention with their rendition of *Joy to The World,* followed by more upbeat Christmas music.

The next day, I reported my lost bank cards and took steps to get a replacement identification card.

On Tuesday, my sister-in-law called.

"Fiona, did you lose something?"

"Lose something?" I echoed, the wallet out of my thoughts by then.

"Yes. A lady called here and said you should call her. She found something of yours."

"Oh yes! I did lose my purse. Did she leave a number?"

"Yes. Do you have a pen?"

After recording the lady's name and number, I called the number immediately.

A woman answered the telephone. "May I speak with Joy, please?"

"This is Joy. How may I help you?"

"Hi Joy. I am Fiona. I heard you may have found something that belongs to me."

"What did you lose?"

"A wallet."

"Describe it."

"It's a black and brown Fendi wallet; about 6" x 6" and fairly new. My coworker bought it for me about two weeks ago while she was in Miami."

"Did it contain money and if so, how much?"

"Yes. About $80.00."

She paused then eventually asked,

"When and where can you meet me to collect it?"

"At 5:00 p.m. this evening at Fairchild Street Bus Terminal, by the newsstand."

"You got it!" she said.

As was planned, I headed to the bus terminal and waited beside the newsstand. It was 4:54 p.m.

Less than two minutes later a tall woman, as brown as the Congo River, with a slight smile on her lips, approached me.

"I guess you are Fiona," she said, her hand outstretched to shake mine.

"Yes, I am. Thank you so very much for returning my purse."

"Don't thank me, thank my husband."

"Why?" I inquired.

"Do you have any idea how expensive that purse is and how pretty it is? I didn't want to return it. After finding the purse, I took it home and showed it to my husband, and I told him I would keep it. He asked me if it contained identification, and I said yes. He said I would do no such thing because he was a police officer, and his job was to uphold the law. He instructed me to return the purse and its contents. He told me to look you up in the telephone directory. I did, but I didn't find your name, so I called another Maughn who said she was your sister-in-law. That's why you are getting your purse back today," she finished, smiling.

"I am thankful that the Lord showed it to you. I prayed, asking Him to help me find it and to hide it from eyes that would want to keep it. I don't know why I prayed the way I did, but God answered my prayer. You found it, and even though you wanted to keep it, your husband convinced you to change your mind. Please thank him too."

On walking away, I praised God for hearing my prayers and returning my purse.

CHAPTER ELEVEN

"…. For your Father knows the things you have need of, before you ask him."

Matthew. 6:8.

Elijah was a mighty man of God. First Kings 16-19 tells of some of the great miracles God performed through him. According to James 5:17-18, it was Elijah who prayed, and the Lord stopped the rain for three and a half years. He prayed at the end of that time and the rain returned. It was Elijah who prayed and called fire down from heaven in the presence of the people who worshipped Baal, the false god. Elijah even turned the sword on Baal's worshippers and slayed thousands.

Elijah was now on a high with God. Not only had he witnessed fire come down from heaven, but after his prayer for rain, he saw a cloud that signaled an impending downpour. Elijah wanted to get to his destination quickly, so he ran the entire way and got down the mountain ahead of Ahab's chariot.

King Ahab told his wife, Jezebel, all the great things Elijah had done, including how he killed the false prophets. She sent a message to Elijah telling him that by the next day, just as he killed Baal's prophets, she would take his life too. Elijah's mountaintop experience now hit a valley low. He was physically exhausted and depressed by the fact that the people demonstrated no immediate change even though they saw God's power on display on Mount Carmel. What do you think that mighty man of God who had just performed wonders on His behalf did? He ran! Not only that – he asked God to take his life. Like some of us might have done, after that talk with God, he probably curled up in the fetal position and fell asleep crying.

It was while Elijah slept that fitful sleep that God showed up for him and ministered to him so that he would have the strength to carry out another task, *even before he (Elijah) called*. First Kings 19:1-8 records how God provided food for Elijah twice in the same day while he was sleeping. On both occasions, Elijah never talked about food, neither did he ask God for food. Isaiah 65:24 records, "And it shall come to pass, that before they call, I will answer . . ." God saw ahead of time that Elijah would have to make a 40-day journey - a journey of which he was unaware and for which he was unprepared, prior to lying down under the juniper tree. God used an angel to supply Elijah's need for food before he even had the opportunity to ask.

Consequently, Elijah was strengthened so that he could perform the task God had for him. This story reminds us that God sees and knows everything. He who knows the end from the beginning, knows our deepest needs and is willing and able to supply them, whatever they are, *even before we call.* I am about to testify to you of how God saw my need and answered, even before I called on Him. He remains the same yesterday, today, and forever. You can trust Him, too!

Even Before I Prayed

After a warm shower, I sat on the edge of the twin bed in the cluttered bedroom of the apartment I shared with my friend in Barbados. I was due at work in two hours. Towel-drying my hair, my eyes came to rest on the faded blue jeans and the well-worn peach top I laid out on the bed. Even my blue floral towel seemed a dingy white, and the flowers had disappeared. *I sure do need some new clothes, shoes, toiletries, and everything, but there's no money.* I sighed deeply. Then my mind wandered to my homeland of Guyana, South America, thousands of miles away. There, I had left my two children. The memory was bittersweet, yet more bitter than sweet.

> *Dear God, take care of my two babies while I'm away. Help them not to forget me and make a way for us to be reunited very soon,* I prayed.

Tears stung my eyelids at the onslaught of painful memories of a shattered marriage and the day I walked away from it all. Even though it was nearly 14 months since that dreadful day, whenever I thought of William, it was as if an electric knife was unceasingly cutting away at my heart. I still loved him. Moving to Barbados and leaving my children behind was the toughest decision of my life. My intention was to get them as soon as I was settled. Yet I was far from being settled.

While working as a project secretary in Georgetown, Guyana, I never thought that one day I would be scrubbing floors, washing pots and pans and cleaning washrooms to make ends meet. Seven and a half years earlier, I had fallen madly in love with the dashing gospel singer, William Larrier, and didn't stop to consider what I was doing when I agreed to give him my hand in marriage. Yes, I had prayed about it, but this was one of the times when I didn't wait to find out whether my partner was the Lord's will for my life. I purposely ignored all the red flags. I was too busy defying my parents, who had said years before that it wasn't the right time to get married. They said I should have been focusing on my studies. I smiled wryly, thinking about the first two years of our courtship and marriage. We met at a church concert and both of us had a passion for music, even though on opposite sides of the spectrum: he was the musician while I just loved music. I couldn't carry a tune in a bucket.

I thought William was all I could hope for in a man, but within less than a year of being married, the honeymoon was over, and he started showing his true colors. By then, I was nearly five months pregnant with our first child. William forsook his Christian principles, started partying, and neglected both his physical and financial duties as a husband and father. Being a Christian wife, I continually prayed for my husband and vowed never to give up on him. Despite the prayers, the situation grew progressively worse. He began drinking. I cringed at the memory of one of the beatings I received at his hands. The chiming of the musical clock interrupted my wandering thoughts with the melody of "Old McDonald Had a Farm" indicating that it was 9:00 a.m.

"Shoot! I gotta get out of here. I'll be late if I don't hurry," I said.

I jumped up and hurriedly started dressing. Taking my only pair of shoes from the closet, I stopped and sighed. Both heels had started wearing down and there was no money for the cobbler, let alone money to purchase a new pair. The $80 wage I made weekly barely paid for my rent, travel expenses and meager food bill. Whenever I sent money to my parents for my children, I could scarcely afford it. *Gosh, I wish I had money as I used to have in Guyana.* Heading out of the house, my mind wandered to Guyana again.

It was as if I had moved from one stage of my life to another — from having enough and always helping others, to barely making it and wearing rags. Back in Guyana, funds were adequate most of the time, and I believed in Luke 6:38 which said, "Give, and it shall be given unto you; good measure, pressed down, and shaken together and running over, shall men give into your bosom. For with the same measure that ye meet withal it shall be measured to you again." I always enjoyed sharing and giving to others. Through the concept of giving, I learned a secret: when I had much and shared, it didn't feel like I did anything; it was when I barely had enough for myself, or when I was down to my last and offered it to someone in need, that I felt as if I gave. Whenever I was generous with my last, I always experienced an inner joy and satisfaction that was beyond explanation.

But there I was, on a foreign island with no family and just a few friends. I knew I needed to pray that God would supply my financial needs, but I put off praying and subsequently forgot.

Two days later, I made my way home after a tiring day at work. My hands were sore, and my back ached. Thursdays were the most strenuous. I mopped the entire four-bedroom house, did dishes, and the ironing for a family of four adults. All in five hours! Opening the door to the apartment, I saw a pink card lying on the carpet. Realizing the mailman must have slipped it under the door and being too tired to even bend down to pick it up, I stepped over it, threw my bag on a chair, eased my shoes from my sore feet, and flopped down on the nearest sofa.

Hours later, light flooded the room. When I opened my eyes, Dawn, my roommate, was standing next to me reading the card.

Looking out the open windows, I noticed it was dark outside.

"Wow! I must have slept for hours," I said, yawning and stretching.

"You got mail, a parcel at the post office for pickup," Dawn said, handing me the card.

"A parcel? What parcel?" I asked.

"I don't know. You not expecting anything?"

"No, I'm not," I replied.

And it doesn't even say who it's from," Dawn said, turning the card around.

"I wonder what that is. I may have to pay to get it, right?"

"But of course, it will cost something," Dawn responded.

I got up, went to the bedroom, put the card on the vanity and forgot about it. Having to pay to collect the package wasn't a thrilling thought, even though I didn't know how much it would cost. The next day was payday, but it was also the weekend my rent was due, so I put off picking up the parcel.

One week later, on the following payday, I went to the post office. I gave the card to the customs clerk who went in search of the parcel. He returned, struggling with a large cardboard box that had my name printed in black on the side and top. I became excited. As soon as he put the box down, I peered at the top, and smiled when I saw the sender's name: Marcel Quinn. *What a pleasant surprise! How come Marcel didn't tell me she was sending me something.*

"I have to check this, madam," the clerk's husky voice interrupted my thoughts.

"Go right ahead," I said, stepping back.

Watching the clerk open the parcel, my mind wandered to Marcel, my old friend from school. Marcel was living in New York, but we kept in touch. The clerk began taking a few items out of the box and I covered my mouth, trying to suppress a scream. It was unbelievable! The clerk was removing clothes and tediously feeling his way between the items in the tightly packed box.

"This will be eight dollars, madam," he said a few minutes later.

Oh, my goodness! And only $8.00! I could have picked it up last week!

"Okay," I said, fishing into my purse and handing him a crisp $10 bill.

"It's heavy. You need help?" the clerk asked.

"Thanks. I'll get a cab and you may help me with it."

Half an hour later, I was sitting on the bedroom floor, with items from the box scattered around me. There was everything in that box that a woman could need and much more. Even though I had forgotten to pray about the things I needed, God, who is always faithful, had seen my need and supplied it, even before I made the time to ask Him. It also seemed as if a divine or miraculous hand had done the packing, because when I was finished unpacking, there was no way that I could fit all the items back into the box. There were several casual and elegant outfits, jeans, underwear, towel sets, toiletries, cologne, casual and dress shoes, bedroom slippers, belts, scarves - the list of items my friend sent me was unending.

I gave thanks to God and started writing my friend a letter, as making international calls was a rarity at that time. Best of all, I was overjoyed to be able to share my gifts with my friend, Dawn, and even mailed some items to my sisters in Guyana. Keep trusting God! He is always looking out for you and will answer *even before you pray*!

CHAPTER TWELVE

***But my God shall supply all your need according
to his riches in glory by Christ Jesus.***

Philippians 4:19

Philippians 4:19 alludes to the fact that *God shall supply all your need according to His riches in glory.* God is a limitless God and while His Word tells us He is able to supply all of our need, it must be noted that this scripture does not merely mean financial need. It also includes any material, spiritual and physical need, that is, any and all need.

By no means is this scripture promoting the prosperity gospel where some believe that God is like a money tree in their backyards. Further, we must also distinguish between a *want* and a *need.* In economics, *need* is defined as something required for survival such as food, water and shelter while *want* is something that people desire, which they may, or may not, be able to obtain. Being the *All-Knowing* God that He is, He knows exactly what we need at any time and will always supply it. Sometimes it may not be what we **think** we need, or we may not even have a need at all, but in His Omniscience, He will supply what He knows is in our best interests.

Psalm 23:1 tells us "The Lord is my Shepherd I shall not want." According to Got Questions Ministries, an online ministry website whose mission is helping people find answers to Bible questions,[2]

---

[2] Got Questions Ministries Phil. 4:19
Is it true that God shall supply all my needs?
https://www.gotquestions.org/my-God-shall-supply-all-my-needs.html

"the secret is knowing we can trust God in every situation." Further, we can say, "My God shall supply all my need," because day by day God gives us the grace and strength to meet every new challenge…" He also reminds us in 2 Corinthians 9:8 that "God is able to bless you abundantly, so that in all things at all times, having all that you need you will abound in every good work." If we go to God, even in our weakest, neediest moments, He supplies the grace and power we need to follow and serve Him and endure adversity.

We must trust God enough to know that He has our best interests at heart and will always keep His promises. In this testimony, I will show you how I had a need – albeit not a critical one – so I called on God, and He showed up, just as He promised He would.

"Pick up the Receiver"

It was sometime in March 2002. I had just moved to the United States from Barbados and had two part-time jobs. My second part-time job was cleaning. Sometimes I would clean at night and might not get home until after 11:00 p.m. On this night, I left work and made my way to the 69th Street terminal in the West Philadelphia, Pennsylvania area to await the El Train.

I suddenly felt the urge to check in on my children. Because my husband would sometimes get in late as well, I wasn't sure if he was there with them. Neither of us had cell phones, and I desperately needed assurance that they were safe. The cold, dark night offered no comfort. It cost a quarter to make a telephone call from the public telephone booth, but I was broke. All I had was my weekly trans-pass to get me to and from my jobs. Looking at the row of telephone booths lining the wall of the train station, I started talking to God.

Lord, I would like to call my children. I just want to know they are safe.

As soon as I uttered that prayer, I heard the words.

"Pick up the receiver."

Quickly I looked around, thinking someone had joined me. There was no one. *But I didn't even vocalize my thoughts.* Realizing that the closest person stood about 12 feet away, I dismissed the idea. A few minutes later the urgent desire to speak with my children overcame me.

Lord, I prayed again, *I would like to speak with my children. Please keep them safe.*

"Pick up the receiver."

It was the same quiet voice. I looked around, but still no one was near enough to have spoken and have me hear.

"Pick up the receiver," the voice said again. This time with a sense of urgency.

I began taking some purposeful steps towards the row of pay phones. Upon reaching them, I looked around.

"Pick up the receiver."

Extending my arm, I picked up the receiver. As soon as I lifted it from its cradle, I heard a coin dropping into the coin box. My heart started racing. I placed the receiver to my ear. There was dial tone! I couldn't believe what I was hearing. Quickly I started dialing my home telephone number. My husband was at the other end of the line.

"Hey! What time are you getting in?" he asked.

"Soon. Are the children, okay?"

"Yes, they' all sleeping."

"You wouldn't believe what just happened," I said.

"What?" he asked.

"I just made a call at the phone booth with no money!"

"Huh?"

"The train is pulling in now. I will talk with you when I get in."

During my train ride home I smiled, thanking God for His faithfulness. At the train station, I had a dire need to ensure that my children were safe. I took a step of faith, obeyed His voice, although skeptically, picked up the receiver and He came through for me. Is there something in your life about which you need to petition God? Are you supposed to be stepping out in faith so you can see Him work for you? Go ahead! Step out! God keeps His promises—He cannot lie!

The End.

Acknowledgements

In the words of Fanny J. Crosby: *To God be the glory, great things He has done!* This is all about God! I can do *nothing* without Him; all the praise, honor and glory are His! Psalm 50:15 reminds me that I can call on God in the day of trouble; He said He would deliver me, and I will glorify Him. God, thank you for loving me and thank you for the relationship you afford me to have with you.

To my husband, Grantley O. Harewood and my children, Donissa, Delon & De-Ann: Your support is matchless. A mere, '*Thank you*' cannot express my gratitude.

To my sister, Shondel Dublin: Your invaluable support and critiques mean a lot.

To my mother and siblings, Rawle, Deon, Junior, Collin, and Darren and my in-laws, nephews, and nieces: Thank you for your support.

To my brother, and sister-in-Christ, Malcolm & Shane O'Dean: Your friendship and encouragement mean the world to me.

To my prayer partner, Rhonda Harding: Thank you for your friendship, fellowship, and those hours we spend talking to and about God and studying His Word. For the tears and laughter, we are sharing on this journey. It's been 10 years, girl!

To my former pastor and friend, Dr. Donald McKinney: Thank you for penning my Foreword and for the confidence you have placed in me over the years.

To Pleasant Street SDA Church's Prayer Group, led by Mrs. Vivienne Morana: I was invited to participate for a month, and we've been hanging out and praying together for six years now. Thank you for persevering in prayer for my family, for and with me.

To my readers: Thank you for endorsing my manuscript, sharing my book with friends and family, and providing reviews. For those of you who have a personal relationship with God, my prayer is that you will continually trust Him, see where He is leading and follow. If you do not know Him personally, my prayer is that you would give Him your hand without further delay. I guarantee you'll wonder what took you so long.

About the Author

Fiona Harewood always wanted to be an author, but never really thought it possible until she started working as a part-time housekeeper for Karen E. Quinones Miller, bestselling author of *Satin Doll* and other novels. One day while washing dishes, she told Miller of her dream. "Put together what you have, and I'll critique it and let you know," Miller told her. And so, it began!

Prior to embarking on her dream career, Harewood, who grew up in Guyana, South America, struggled in high school. Before migrating to the United States in February 2001, she lived in Barbados, West Indies, for thirteen years and worked in the airline industry.

After living in the United States for a few years, she decided that she didn't want to be a housekeeper anymore, but her limited education prevented her from obtaining the types of jobs she desired. So, at age 44 she went back to school. She has since earned a Bachelor of Science degree in Paralegal Studies and a Master's degree in Public Policy from Peirce College and Drexel University, respectively.

While in college, Harewood was astounded by the dropout statistics which she describes as an epidemic. She reasoned that if she was able to complete her education, others could do it, too. Consequently, she chose to investigate the dropout situation in the United States for her master's thesis. Thereafter, she made a commitment to motivate students to persevere as they navigated their educational journeys and to challenge dropouts to become dream makers. This was the impetus for her first book – *I Did It, You Can, Too!*

Harewood's public appearances have included interviews on the Urban Connections, Beacon of Light, and Breakthrough Success Podcasts, as well as Targeted Podcasts True Crime Domestic Violence and guest appearances on the National Communications Network (NCN) and Channel 9 News, abroad.

Harewood is a federal employee. When she's not functioning in that capacity, she conducts motivational workshops and seminars encouraging victims of abuse to rise above their circumstances, inspiring young people to stay in school and challenging dropouts to become dream-makers. She lives in Philadelphia, Pennsylvania with her husband and has three adult children.

 www.fionaharewood.com

 fiona@fionaharewood.com

 FHarewood

 facebook.com/fiona-harewood

 instagram.com/fionaharewood   youtube.com/c/FionaHarewoodHopePublishers

Heartfelt gratitude to the Writing with Purpose Group:

Bridgette Bastien is a child of God, a wife, and a mother of two beautiful daughters. She is also the author of three books – *Overcomer, S-Factor,* and *Remember* – in the *Prayer Saved My Life* series. Writing a book was never on her bucket list until she was snatched from the jaws of death. After that experience, Bastien reignited a desire to share the life-changing power of prayer and to celebrate the saving grace of God with others.

Bastien's third book, *Remember,* will be released in late 2022. It is biblically based, packed with unforgettable stories and enriched by extraordinary encounters. *Remember* highlights how pivotal the past is to our present and future. Professionally, she was a research chemist early in her career, holds a Master's in Strategy and Marketing from the Wharton School of Business – University of Pennsylvania, and is now a marketing professional.

Bastien lives in Massachusetts with her family and is an active member of Pleasant Street SDA Church. She leads the Youth Sabbath School Ministry and plays a vital role in the Prayer and Women's Ministries at her church. She feasts on the Bible and, according to her daughters, "She has playdates with her prayer group three times per day." She loves traveling the world, eating spicy foods, and basking in the warmth of her family and friends' love.

Contact Bastien and learn more about her *Prayer Saved My Life* Ministry:

 www.prayersavedmylife.com

 Prayersavedmylife@gmail.com

 instagram.com/prayersavedmylife

 facebook.com/prayersavedmylife

Nathan Stephens is an innovative professional with a personal track record of delivering a comprehensive portfolio of services and results-oriented solutions designed to help align people (which is the most important component), processes, and technology. His strengths include a demonstrated capability in implementing technology solutions, developing best-in-class information system governance models and the ability to effectively interface with senior executives to develop and measure strategic goals and objectives.

With 20+ years of professional IT Service Delivery experience - the last 3 years with an International Infrastructure process flow focus – he has primarily worked very closely with CIOs and IT executives in various organizations to "avoid majoring in the minor issues" and plotting both strategic solutions and tactical plans for IT services recovery, performance optimization, and business integration. He lets the data lead him to the problem that needs to be solved.

Nathan maintains a balance of client-facing delivery work and internal business operational process management. He has been responsible for infrastructure and service delivery, overseeing system administration and client support, and has held cross-functional roles in sales, pre-sales, alliances, and marketing. He is a customer advocate throughout all aspects of the customer lifecycle supported by Lean Six Sigma methodologies.

The attribute that leads to Nathan's sustainability within any origination is that he never takes his focus off the customer's expectations.

Fiona Harewood

Coming Soon!

Prayer to the Rescue Series – *Book Two*
Protection Around a Period of Time

Special Thanks to my Editors:

Rhonda Harding is a native of Trinidad, and holds a bachelor's degree in elementary education, a master's degree in special education, and a certificate of advanced graduate studies in school administration and supervision. She enjoys good books, good jokes, good friends, and good food. She also enjoys writing; editing is her passion. She resides in Maryland with her son, Christian.

Lahai McKinnie is a ministerial wife and mother to three school-aged children. She has a passion for writing and editing and holds over 20 years of professional and freelance experience in the field. She holds degrees in both journalism and social work and is based in central Pennsylvania. When she isn't working, she enjoys taking walks in nature and being in the company of friends.

www.ingramcontent.com/pod-product-compliance
Lightning Source LLC
Chambersburg PA
CBHW071924290426
44110CB00013B/1471